DYSFUNCTIONAL FAMILIES CAN CHANGE

PALMETTO
PUBLISHING
Charleston, SC
www.PalmettoPublishing.com

Unless otherwise noted Scripture verses are from the New International Version, copyright ©1973, 1978, 1984 by International Bible Society. Used by permission of Zondervan. All rights reserved.

Scripture quotations marked "NASB" are from the New American Standard Bible®, Copyright © 1960, 1962, 1963, 1968, 1971, 1972, 1973,1975, 1977, 1995 by The Lockman Foundation. Used by permission. (www.Lockman.org)

Scripture quotations marked NKJV are taken from the New King James Version®. Copyright © 1982 by Thomas Nelson. Used by permission. All rights reserved.

Scripture quotations marked "NLT" are taken from the Holy Bible, New Living Translation, copyright 1996. Used by permission of Tyndale House Publishers, Inc., Wheaton, Illinois 60189. All rights reserved.

Paperback ISBN: 979-8-8229-3172-5
eBook ISBN: 979-8-8229-3173-2

From the Heart
of a Local Church Pastor

DYSFUNCTIONAL FAMILIES CAN CHANGE

J. RICHARD HORNER

Endorsements

Experience is such a great teacher. In, *"Dysfunctional Families Can Change"*, Rick draws from his many years of pastoral ministry to engage some of the important relational and social issues that families confront today. Firmly based in the scriptures, he draws from his years of experience to pen appropriate counseling application for pastors and lay leaders today. This book is not theory - it is application.

Pastor Brian McCall, Sr. Pastor
Martinsburg Grace Brethren Church
Formerly Vocational Technical Coordinator
@ Federal Correction Institution, Loretto, PA

The impact of family dysfunction is evident in every classroom as children struggle for stability, in every counselor's office as clients battle with anxiety and depression, in every workplace as co-workers "stuff" makes it hard to collaborate in healthy ways, and in every church as folks have trouble differentiating a heavenly Father and church family from an earthly parent and dysfunction at home. But, God takes the brokenness and redeems it. He puts the pieces back together. There is hope. You'll find it in every chapter of this book. With Biblical exposition, marital wisdom, and a pastoral heart, Pastor Rick Horner will help you along the path of change.

Bruce Barlow, Pastor
broken home overcomer,
and strong family advocate

Rick Horner can help us know how to approach and actually help people in need in their families. This book fills an important gap between books by exemplary experts and testimonies by people who have thrived in spite of all the challenges at home. You will feel, as I do, that Rick is coming alongside to help and that he knows what he's talking about both biblically and in terms of the situations we face.

Dr. John Teevan Current Co-Dean
of the School of Arts and Humanities.
Grace College & Seminary,
Winona Lake, IN
Former Executive Director of the
Grace College Prison Extension
in Indiana State Prisons

"I have been in pastoral ministry for over 20 years and have seen first hand the pain of dysfunctional families. This book offers helpful insights about how to minister to those who carry unseen hurts. Rick has been sharing the grace of God with hurting people for many decades and this resource tool will be of tremendous benefit to those who want to do the same."

Pastor Mark Lingenfelter Sr. Pastor
Grace Fellowship Church

Pastor Horner takes everything we know about the brain disease of substance use disorder and its link to generational trauma and applies it through a Biblical lens in this book. It is an encouraging and educational read for anyone in the Christian faith!"

Natalie Kauffman Exec. Director
Cambria County Drug Coalition,
Johnstown, PA

We are all acquainted with dysfunctional families—we might even be in one. We are the beneficiaries of Horner's years of pastoral experience with just such families, culminating in this book. Using his proven methods will enable pastors and counselors to help restore troubled families to wholeness.

Jesse Deloe, Author & Editor

This essential guide for pastors and laymen provides support and assistance in dealing with the increasing numbers and issues of dysfunctional families. It Biblically illustrates the application of grace and forgiveness that today's society so desperately needs.

Pastor Philip J. Waite
M.Ed/TheoLead Pastor
and President of
Target One Ministries Inc

Acknowledgements

I know I could not have done this important project without the assistance of several significant friends, members, and most importantly my amazing GOD – who put this whole idea on my heart..

First, I want to thank author and editor Jesse Deloe! When I first asked him for help, he must have seen something in my earnestness that stirred him to guide and encourage me during the long editing process. Then my special friend, Pastor Brian McCall has stayed with me for the long haul in critiquing and challenging me to put my thoughts down and tell my stories the best way.

Then there were advisors like Urban Missionary John Shirk and Senior Pastor Bruce Barlow and retired Pastor Jim Laird who queried my wording and kept me on task to share my experiences where they fit right. Pastor, Administrator and College professor Dr. John Teevan encouraged my writing style. And Psychologist Noah Cicalo corrected my grammar as well as enhanced and confirmed my learning on peoples' emotions and how they often do not handle them.

Senior Pastor Mark Lingenfelter supported my plan to help dysfunctional families and graciously offered his pluses and minuses about what I covered in the treatise. Also, Professors Dr. David Van Dyke and Dr. Thomas Edgington, plus Pastors Tim Sprankle and Phil Waite all added insight to specific chapters in my manuscript.

Then I want to thank Mr. John Funk and my daughter Jessica Husted for their time consuming work of proofreading and continual editing of my book in the later stages. Yet most of all, the biggest help came from my precious wife who challenged my proposals, kept me on task, made sure my stories were right, guided some of my grammar, corrected my typing, and blessed my work in her own unique ways. So glad God put us together 53 years ago; and enabled us to serve HIM together as an effective team for the last 49!

Preface

THE PURPOSE OF THIS BOOK

Dysfunctional Families are destroying the fabric of our nation. It is in the family that people learn how to live with others. God launched the world with a family. Everyone comes from or has a family. So, to some degree, most all of us learn and understand the concept of taking care of and doing for one another by personal experience. Some realize this in a positive light, but others know the pain of little care and the misery of not being blessed by another person.

I believe the purpose of the family is to learn how to love, care about, provide for, and cope with others who are brought into our lives through circumstances beyond our control. So, forming, establishing, and perfecting relationships becomes the way people learn how to progress in time and develop life skills. The family is our training ground.

For many reasons we can pass or fail in this school of association. In my experience in dealing with people, I have learned there are many influences in the world that work to destroy proper and godly relationships. Just as an individual needs help in overcoming personal sin, so we

" The family is our training ground "

all need assistance in halting the declension of kinship or dealing with the unnatural pain of not being loved.

Because of their inborn sin nature, individuals quickly come to believe that they themselves are the most important people around. The more one focuses on that analysis, the quicker he or she decides that families can be jettisoned. The atmosphere in America today is fertile ground not only for rebuffing relationships at home but repudiating the necessity of keeping close connections with members of the original household. Today's tough society highlights the feeling, "I can, and I will do it myself!"

For these reasons I have researched and reexamined the unfortunate emergence of the dysfunctional family. Through the last six decades, as life has become more immoral, self-centered, greedy, and cruel, the loving and supporting early life in a home has rapidly disappeared in most urban centers and countless rural communities of our America. The once stable nuclear family has been broken. I am writing with a plea and a persuasion to right the ship and repair the unsound foundation; or more directly, to carefully and biblically replace the rotted base materials of households.

I believe with God's help and the principles explained here, relief and renovation are definite possibilities with the chaotic households that surround the reader. As you peruse this treatise, you may become discouraged. That is okay. You might be shocked with my statistics or saddened by my stories. I would expect that. You may even get angry at my explanation for the causes and hidden reasons that families fall apart. That would fulfill part of my purpose. Yet my hope is that, as you work through my planned explanation and determined proposal, you will feel an overwhelming desire to get involved. Lives are being ruined;

people are living in great emotional pain and hateful anger, often contemplating foolish or dangerous choices. This is happening right next to us every day. The wounded are in our churches and the helpless and hopeless are in our schools and factories.

Someone must rise up and make a difference. Believers must take the baton and run the race of bearing their burdens (Galatians 6:2). God's servants must allow HIM to use them as spiritual and emotional healers. Perhaps in the field where the harvest is plentiful, YOU are the worker being prayed for (Matthew 9:37). Just maybe that is why you are reading this book.

In "Dysfunctional Families Can Change", I feel the Lord has led me to five main propositions that Christian counselors, youth pastors, active elders, and mature Christian community leaders can use to help mend broken people. We must first understand the problem, defining the "Dysfunctional Family." Then, I seek to show how disrupted or even destroyed families can be redeemed. It will be worth the work of learning of the "sin nature" and "self-esteem". In the third Unit I point out how God's Holy Spirit can lead us to lovingly counsel hurting families living around us to find hope, forgiveness, and even power. For the mind is a battleground. *We must go to the Scriptures to find how to keep damaging thoughts from forming negative strongholds that keep our families defeated!*

Then comes the hard and deliberate biblical work toward victory. I set out a strong pattern of a "Healthy Home" to use as a guide, and then I discuss the reasons why suffering often occurs without such guidelines, and how the Lord can help people through trials. This involves finding ways to use the many current resources that are available to churches and communities in our hopeful nation. Many family counseling books do not show how individual churches (small or large) can be influential in reestablishing relationships and building confidence and courage in households that have given up on experiencing personal acceptance, value, and future potential. Then the 5th proposition is a summary of what motivates people like us to sacrifice our time and talent and learn more of Christ's compassion to rescue God's sheep who are "harassed and helpless" (Matthew 9:36).

To give you some additional information to prepare you to make the most of this book, let me explain each unit a little better.

Unit I: EXPOSING the PROBLEM has three chapters that define what a dysfunctional family is. I uncover flawed parenting, the four forced roles of children, and the Deuteronomy 5: 9 Principle that explains some of the reasons why children get hurt badly. Also included is how the devil's three temptations affect each of the four types of flawed parents - big reasons why dads and moms fail.

Unit II: SAVING the FAMILY is the section where we talk about the soul and how personal sin has affected it. From there I give some history of how the devil has attacked our nation and our individual families. Then I finish the unit discussing Jesus' power to rebuild the family. I will explain the importance of parental boundaries and the significance of poor self-esteem among battered children.

Unit III: POWER to CHANGE the FAMILY. We clearly need the Holy Spirit's guidance in learning about *agape* love, and how it can work in changing relationships. The need to find forgiveness is crucial. One of my most important arguments is that forgiveness can set the wounded free in most families better than anything else. The last chapter of this unit points out that negative strongholds in the mind must be identified and captured by Christ. This will enable victory over bad habits and wrong patterns that have developed in the first and second, and even third generations of broken families.

Unit IV: VICTORY for the DYSFUNCTIONAL FAMILY. Here is what the Healthy and Functional Family can look like, and it's a model for us to strive towards. Chapter 11 offers a four-point plan, using words starting with the letter P. These represent strides in action that God can develop in peoples' hearts to rebuild the collapse that has taken place. Plus, we help our counselees discover their suffering was part of God's plan to give them victory over the calamity they went through. I close this section with a seven-step procedure for local churches to use in restoring families in their communities.

Unit 5: SUMMARY from a PASTOR'S HEART is the final section where I incorporate my work with the drug war in the town where I spent my last eight years of ministry before I retired. Dealing with dysfunctional families in that environment provided me with lots of experience and a fresh motivation to lift up as many people as God would allow. I relearned how to use my problem-solving personality and the God-placed urgency to win souls in dealing with families in the terrible trap of the street drug culture. The Lord taught me more about His compassion so I could share it now with my readers.

About a year before publishing my book, I was explaining it to a curious recent high school graduate. He was a Christian teen near and dear to me. As I described the impact of the "Controlling Father" and how his critical traits pass down to and through his kids, this young man suddenly responded,

That's what my dad went through. My Grandad was that way. I can see some of those negative traits in my father. He wanted to be right all the time; he forced his will on us. And he still has a temper. But when

Dad was saved, he really changed. He is very loving and did a great job in raising us unselfishly. It's interesting to know that my dad suffered through a somewhat universal family issue. I'll be happy to read your book when it's finished.

This young adult's positive real-life recognition was great to see. Knowing his family, I could confirm his discovery. That encounter stirred me on to finish my research and complete my analysis and proposals.

I also want to mention one of the unique ways I chose to write this book. After pointing out different trends and truths that I experienced in ministry, *I make some important observations about how you, the reader, can use the lessons I learned. My suggestions of what you could do in similar circumstances* <u>will appear in italics</u> in the following pages. So, guidelines for counseling are printed differently from the regular text.

With a great desire to honor the God who sent me and accomplished things through me, I took the liberty to capitalize the pronouns HE and HIS in the printing. We serve an amazing God, and HE deserves to be highlighted and uplifted as much as we can!

So, I trust as you read this material describing the ministry of my wife and me over 40 years as pastor and wife to six evangelical and conservative churches (note more personal details in the Introduction and Chapter 13) that you will see how our gracious God used us. I believe HE led us to teach the Bible, counsel people going through difficult marriages, and lead people of all ages to a saving relationship with Jesus Christ. HE used us to love on and firmly guide teenagers, help individuals and families deal with addiction to controlled substances, and disciple new and struggling believers to know and follow Christ in real and living ways.

This is who God made me to be. You are invited then to see how my Savior and Lord worked through me to develop the 10 principles in this book:

- Realizing and using God's Compassion for the wandering and harassed
- Recognizing the causes and issues of the Dysfunctional Family in America
- Standing up to and combating Satan with the Word of God
- Emphasizing the necessity of repenting from personal sin
- Learning how to apply God's "Agape Love" to family relationships
- Understanding the significant individual Power of Forgiveness
- Battling the negative Strongholds that form in our minds and souls
- Accepting the difficulties of past suffering, then allowing God to work
- Considering the impact of a Local Church Plan for helping needy families
- Building urgency to believe that the people the Lord sends us can be changed!

Thanks for spending time scanning, reading, studying, or using these principles! May God use them through you to bring people to HIM and to expand HIS strong Kingdom!

Pastor John Richard Horner
A seeking and trusting Servant of the Master

Introduction

MINISTERING TO DYSFUNCTIONAL FAMILIES

I am amazed that God has used me as a local church pastor for 45 years. The Lord has placed my wife and me in six different locations to spread the powerful Word of God and to share His amazing love with people in small towns, suburban areas, and inner-city ministries in Northeastern and Mid-Atlantic sections of the United States. In my call to ministry in 1975, the Lord impressed me to take seriously working with lost people and bringing them to a saving knowledge of Jesus and then showing them how to become better individuals.

HE had begun that process in me three years earlier. I just could not get over Jesus' great love for me as demonstrated on the cross; and that my new Father God wanted me to share with others just like myself. This complete change of thinking and earnest pursuing at age 22 was real and burning in my soul. I had no idea what it would entail for the future, especially the raising of my young family of daughters.

My marriage had started with difficulty - great on love but short on giving. Married life had unearthed big challenges. So, without a job, quitting college, and having children too soon, Bettie and I had little idea of what it meant to sacrifice in a relationship. Nor did we understand what raising a family would mean. When we were about to give up, Jesus Christ spoke to both of us about our individual sin – past and present. We sincerely repented for both the messes we had made of our own lives, and how we had hurt each other with our selfishness! Then we gradually allowed HIM to show us what the penetrating words from Philippians 2:3 could mean for us. We learned that by ceasing to do things out of "selfish ambition or vain conceit" we could humbly consider each other "more important than ourselves" (NASB).

This principle suddenly made good sense; and that verse became individual goals for us and our young family. Shortly after, we discovered that GOD had special plans not only for our eternal souls, but also to work on our spiritual lives here on earth. That is how the Lord kept us from becoming foolish parents and crippling our precious children. Next, HE led us to a strong Bible-believing church and taught us how to pursue this new passion that HE had given both of us - to exercise sacrificial love for strangers. We soon moved to another town. There I worked as a Prudential Insurance agent while God was forming us into pastor and wife of an exciting newly planted Grace Brethren Church.

As we learned a lot in dealing with people, we figured out that family history played a big role in how folks looked at their world and how they reacted to others around them. Before I became a pastor, I had ministered to a new believer with a very difficult up-bringing who was now frightening and even angering his own young kids. (see opening chapter). And now in this small new town where I was sharing the

Gospel, I found many strained relationships between the young adults and teens and their parents. I assumed it was their lost condition without Christ and the destructive things that were happening in America, including the new "sexual revolution" and resistance to authority of the 1960s and 70s. So, I accepted the struggles in families as sin and Satan's bigger impact around our nation (see chapters 3 & 5). Yet in time, I had to learn that a major part of the problem then was how society was creating "Dysfunctional Families" without realizing it.

Then in my second church I discovered through my studies and a personality test that I was a problem solver by nature with a phlegmatic or easy-going temperament. So, I saw my calling expanding to work also with individual couples and to help them strengthen their marriages through a good understanding of how to forgive their mates as well as their parents. As they would allow the Lord to put a new heart and new desire inside, they could all become what they were really intended to be. I felt strongly that we could win many people to Christ this way and quickly overcome the relationship problems as the Holy Spirit began to work on love and forgiveness with the new converts. My wife and I saw several couples come to Christ or return to their "first love" - Jesus. And then, in time, these rejuvenated parents would bring their whole families to church, including the grandparents. That happened in both of our first two congregations (a new small-town work, and then a 100-year-old established city church) as proof that the Word of God changes hearts.

Yet, as decades of ministry flew by, the fissures between the generations seemed to increase in America. I tried to console myself that because of spiritual blindness (2 Corinthians 4:4), the masses were just following the path Jesus spoke of in Matthew 7:13-14, "Wide is the gate, broad the road that leads to destruction, and many enter through it." I felt, however, that somewhere there was a better answer to preserving the family and stopping the downward trend that was taking each generation further and further into misery.

It was not until my last congregation in a small run-down city in Pennsylvania that the needs of families around us became overwhelming. I found myself in the middle of a debilitating opioid and heroin drug culture. This problem was affecting our church, as well as our community. And then, after 40 years of counseling couples and building youth ministries in five different cities and towns, I was finally introduced to the new concept of the "Dysfunctional Family."

I believe in my heart that it is the responsibility of today's church to help broken families who live in our parish areas and neighborhoods. Throughout this book, much vital information is provided on causes for and results of "dysfunctional families". Also, there are sound steps that can be taken by willing biblical counselors of small or large local churches to "take back the city" (at least many of its families) for Jesus!

My parents were divorced in the early 1960s after a few years of screaming, swinging, and then an extra-marital affair. So, my sister and I, as elementary kids, were scared a lot. Both parents tried to comfort us with "It's all right, Rick. We'll work this out." But they did not, and Mom practically abandoned us. Our father did a good job of providing for us, but we got our nurturing from our wonderful grandparents (ironically, but God-ordained) on Mom's side. My response was to forget our problems and look for the good to come, but my sister could not do that. And when Dad remarried a few years later, she could not adjust to our stepmom. After I found Christ as my Savior, I was willing to forgive our wayward mother, but my sister never found peace with her until about two years before our mom's death at age 88. My birth sibling had problems trusting people and having a good self-image most of her life. The pain and peril of dysfunction affected her deeply.

But thanks be to God, my soft heart was made whole early on. And the Holy Spirit has helped me understand the brokenness of adults and the truth that without Christ we are all capable of hurting anyone in our lives. Just as God has forgiven me and washed me clean, I know that I need to forgive other people who have sinned against me. And God can take over and help me to love them despite the unfair past.

I believe the tragedy in my own dysfunctional childhood and the search for real sincere love led me to needing and finding the Lord Jesus. Then HE helped me become more sensitive to the pain that others are going through. I have spent much of my ministry involved with marriage counseling. God has used me to help people before they say, "I do" as well as afterwards when they say, "I don't anymore." I have found that people become much wiser after they see what Scripture says about their own stubbornness and selfishness. And, I have also discovered that most couples respond slowly but favorably to what the Lord says about forgiving and forgetting the sins of their mates. This is especially so when God and His power are brought into the equation. The Gospel and Christ's teachings have changed and continue to change the hearts of people who have been confused or even torn apart inside whether by a mate or a parent.

It is my intention in this treatise to help Christian leaders. As a pastor who had to learn through much trial and error, I strongly desire to explain the condition of dysfunctional families to other pastors and counselors who find themselves working with and advising the grown children of chaotic homes. A large part of our neighbors and even many members of our flocks in this 21st century struggle with how they have been let down in their upbringing. Numerous folks we know have been purposefully abandoned, mistreated, or endangered as kids by adults or older siblings. Plus, there are a lot of young moms and dads who have never been trained to care for and properly nurture babies or toddlers; so, multitudes of people who are young adult now, were without realizing it mentally damaged at a very young age!

It is my desire here to make terms and causes like strongholds, scapegoats, a generational curse, delusion, codependency, and controlling or coddling parents to become common knowledge and familiar vocabulary. You will see I key in on discipleship, relationships, and showing God's love. I'm also trying to teach important spiritual truths like:

- We all need respect and significance from others to handle life well.
- It is possible to understand some reasons why bad things happen.
- There are clear, powerful, and enduring ways right now to salvage broken hearts and to sabotage the wiles of Satan.

It is my hope that there is helpful guidance in this book for both the teachers of biblical truths and the curious students of life. God's Word has the answers! And material like this can make those solutions understandable to both the instructors and the victims. You may have studied or become curious about the deep emotional and mental hurt that mistreated (even sexually or physically abused) children have received while growing up in broken homes or possibly evil foster care or adoption families. Here you will find some beginning aids to comfort people. Plus, I have encouraged further recommended reading in this publication to provide more hope. The writings of many Christian psychologists fill in the specific details that the Bible does not specifically address. I seek here to explain some significant counseling help that I have learned and used to solve serious heart-felt issues. Mature Christians in every church that are willing to learn more about and work with dysfunctional families will be able to show some clear paths for victims. I have also recently gained much insight by working with people in the drug culture for about 4 years. You will read several difficult and succinct illustrations from that complicated and satanic arena!

My book is filled with Bible verse references because I believe Christ is the Answer, and God's Word gives us Jesus' New Testament instructions on relationships despite sinful conditions. The solutions to any of our problems are based on the principles and commands that God shows us. I also seek to emphasize that the Lord is always ready and willing to intervene in our lives. HE wants to show us what HE intended us to be and do as part of HIS colossal gracious design on earth. Mature believers can take what the Holy Spirit says and use it to motivate or rejuvenate the one who turns to HIM. I have been challenged and empowered often through the years with Paul's teaching on the Holy Spirit communing with our spirit about "discerning hidden wisdom and spiritual truths"! (I Corinthians 2:8-16). Let us look at this together!

May God use this book in your life as HE knows best: whether for teachers as instruments for noble purposes or for the listening, wounded souls to recognize that the Spirit of truth really can set them free! (See 2 Timothy 2:20-21 and 1 John 4:6).

UNIT I

EXPOSING THE PROBLEM

Unit I

EXPOSING THE PROBLEM

Everyone is part of a family! Even if you have no siblings, and your parents are gone; at one time you had a mother. Whether your family disowned you or you are avoiding them - you had a start with a parent. The orphan, the homeless, even the reclusive hermit - all had a biological dad and mom in the beginning!

In the book of Genesis all population began with the created man and the woman God fashioned and gave to be his wife. Life started with a family; and male and female "begat" children. So, we all came from someone, not just a mysterious "big bang" or blob somewhere.

Unfortunately, also in the beginning, Satan sought to disrupt, discourage, and destroy the family. His plan was to keep it from accomplishing its original intent, which I will explain in a moment. Yet in the Old Testament God kept track of the generations and succeeded in passing on important truths to the offspring of each chosen couple. And as promised in Genesis 3:15 through the seed of the line of Abraham, the

Messiah came to "crush the serpent's head"! This promise, the Creator's Plan, brought victory to believing mankind and conquered the penalty and power of sin - even in each individual family! With Israel's exodus from Egypt, God spoke through Moses to explain that a major role of the family would be to pass on the words of the Savior to the children, so they would know how-to live-in righteousness, love, and sacrifice.

Because of the sin nature humans have failed to obey and keep those beneficial commandments down through the centuries. Some parents have developed their own idols and rules. Others have determined to write their own stories - without God. Then still additional dads and moms have selfishly and pridefully used "the knowledge of good and evil" to try to become wiser than God. And adding to that sin of idolatry, desiring to be capable of living without the love of a family!

These wicked examples have produced "dysfunctional families" through the centuries; and have caused much havoc, misery, and death around the world. But now in our 21st century America, the damage of living without a caring family has greatly magnified. Plus, in our age of exceedingly foolish knowledge, atheistic scientific accomplishments, and greedy global wealth – we are losing the battle to be strong, helpful, and godly in society! Why? Because the family is broken and chaotic!

So, in these first three chapters I will explain what I think a "Dysfunctional Family" is. Plus, I will point out what I see as the main causes of broken families. I will focus on "Flawed Parents" and Satan's strategy to tempt and ruin adults who have yielded to faulty patterns and prideful life decisions! And we will also start a continual theme of the four distinct roles that kids of Dysfunctional Homes are forced to play.

Chapter 1

A REAL FAMILY WITH A REAL PROBLEM

THE BEGINNING

My friend Jeff had a difficult family life. At an early age he was afraid of his alcoholic father who screamed at his mother and beat her in front of the kids. If anyone resisted, everyone got a shellacking and blood flowed. Psychologically, his mom must have felt that she deserved her physical beatings because she never left home. She may have felt unsafe if she ran, fearing her husband would go out of his way to find her and end her life. Jeff's mom did try to protect, hide, and help the kids, but she did not know how to love them even when the dad wasn't home. Yet, two positive things did happen amid the chaos: Jeff learned from his father how to repair cars and to fend for himself.

Jeff was a slow learner, and kids at school picked on him. As he grew bigger, he won most of the school fights. As a teen, he became muscular and tough, stayed out late, and tried to avoid his father's drunken rages. This was clearly a "dysfunctional family."

Jeff's mother died while he was in middle school, so he had to care for himself. He started to work at the age of 14. He found a sweet, young lady and decided to get married at age 18 (she was 16) and have his own family. The trouble was, neither one of them knew how to take care of a family. So, the man-of-the-house did things the only way he knew how—be boss and make demands.

Despite his limited education, he found that he could make a decent living working on cars. He was a talented handy man at repairing and building things and was as strong as an ox, impressing his customers. But when it came to caring for babies, playing with toddlers, or helping kids with schoolwork, he was at a loss and often was missing from home. He did not know how to sit down and play games with his children or show them how to ride a bike, but he did teach them how to win a fight with the neighbor kids. Giving positive advice and helping with homework as they got into grade school and beyond was out of his league. His wife determined to love on and care for their kids all by herself.

When Jeff was saved at a church service that a neighbor invited him to, he started to look at life differently. He got a new heart. He was now concerned about what God wanted him to do, and he felt like he needed to act as a good and kind person among his new church friends. He also began to feel it was important to provide what was best for his children, an attitude he never had before. However, he expected the adults at church to show the kids how to live and talk correctly. So, because of his own father's bad influence, Jeff still took no responsibility for raising his children. Socially, my family and I enjoyed Jeff's family, but if the kids would fight or something would go wrong, Jeff would be embarrassed and flare up at them and then leave the scene immediately. Although he was more careful now at what words came out of his mouth, he struggled at not showing his temper.

SYMPATHY FOR DYSFUNCTION

Often, I saw his father's cruelty coming through in the way Jeff treated his wife and children. Once Jeff was so irate that he raised his arm to strike his wife, Susan. Instinctively, I jumped between them and almost took the blow, but his fist stopped in mid-air. He struggled to overcome what he learned in his undisciplined and chaotic upbringing in contrast to what he knew needed to be reprogrammed with the power from above. The Holy Spirit was working, but unfortunately, so was the devil.

At the time, I did not understand dysfunctional families. Because I had been raised in a divorced home, and as a sympathetic adult and a pastor of grace, I had a special place in my heart for someone who had experienced an unfair life. I cared about my friend's struggles; yet I could not understand his inability to overcome them despite his having become a born-again Christian.

Although Jeff was amazed at God and HIS plan of forgiveness and understood that it applied to him; it was very difficult for him to forgive those who had hurt him in the past. Because of his vicious childhood struggles and resentment, Jeff had built up hard scales of pride in his heart. So, he constantly imagined that other Christian people were looking down on him because of his lack of knowledge, nice clothing, or newer car to drive. I now see his ups and downs differently.

UNWISE ATTEMPTS TO HELP

On one occasion, Jeff's car broke down and he had no money to fix it. My father-in-law had given us his second car two months earlier, and as we had used it only a few times, I lobbied to give my friend our second vehicle. That did not go over well with my wife or her father. In trying to be extra kind and help my friend, I insisted it was the right thing to do. He needed to see godly love, and I thought that an example of sacrifice on our part would go a long way to help him grow spiritually. I made my wife feel guilty with the Bible verse, "It is more blessed to give than to receive" (Acts 20:35 KJV).

My sincere but misguided empathy was not God's directing. We should have prayed this through together and waited to see what the Lord wanted us to do. God may have had other things in mind to teach Jeff, such as allowing him to suffer a little and to depend on his new Provider more. My generosity could have short-circuited the Lord's plan.

Insisting that we do things my way caused friction in our home. "Besides, God would bless us for it," I said. "Give, and it will be given to you. A good measure, pressed down, shaken together, and running over, will be poured into your lap" (Luke 6:38 NIV). Yet this verse did not fit our situation. We were not in this together, and it was not a "good measure" but an arranged and selfish measure on my part. Nevertheless, at the time, I won. The vehicle was quickly transferred into Jeff's name. Within two weeks, he had sold our car and got a nicer one. I definitely learned a lesson! A person who grew up in a survival-of-the-fittest atmosphere would tend to live that way even as a new Christian adult.

Jeff could not figure out why my wife was miffed. When I told him he should not have sold the car we had sacrificed for him to have, he asked, "Aren't Christians supposed to give the shirt off their back to a fellow believer when they're in need?"

THE POISON OF FAMILY DYSFUNCTION

I did not realize at the time that the man I was trying to disciple was greatly poisoned by the long-reaching problem of dysfunction. We soon lost touch, as I moved away to pastor a church in another state. However, 16 years later we returned to our hometown and remade acquaintances. By this time, Jeff's kids were adults with children of their own. Two of his four kids would not have anything to do with their dad, yet they wanted to visit with and attend to their sickly mother. The adult children were having trouble dealing with their own lives and new families. As a gospel pastor, I understood the Lord wanted me to try to salvage these broken relationships and to lead these young adults to Christ and direct them to a better way to raise their own children.

My first step was to listen to their complaints, hoping to teach them what the Bible says about the power of forgiveness. In the process, I discovered that the older daughter was having marital problems. She had been looking for a man to love her for who she was. Her own father had little skill in affection and could never seem to discuss real life issues with her as a teen. As a result, after two sour relationships and two children, she had not found that missing soul-connection!

In addition, her older brother was trying hard to raise his daughter differently from the way he was handled as a kid. He poured himself into proper discipline, helping her with schoolwork, developing her into a lovely young lady, advising her about dating, talking about her future, and setting her up to attend a Christian college. In the process they had found a good Bible-believing church with a strong youth group. But, after years of quarreling about family issues, this couple was ready for divorce.

As the saying goes, "Like father, like son." Although I did not know the term "dysfunctional family" then, the trap my older friend grew up in had made its demonic way through a second and third generation. I could not help but wonder about the curse God describes in Deuteronomy 5:9 that He will punish the children of the fathers who hate Him (Jeff's Dad), to the third and fourth generation. In time I was to find out just what that meant not only for this household but for all the many descendants caught in dysfunctional families.

Meanwhile, Jeff's struggle with pride and mistrust showed up often as he and his wife moved from one evangelical church to another. Then he settled for staying home on Sundays and enjoying preaching on radio and cassette tape. Still his faith grew, and his domineering feelings toward his adult offspring turned to appreciation. Sadly, he could not understand the anger and disrespect that he had built in the minds of his own children over the years. Through various family events over the next eight years including four weddings, a few difficult hospital trips, and a funeral, the family slowly pulled together and decided to accept one another. With each trial, the Lord's power was shown and some of their lives were changed.

> " *The missing element of love was never shown, and never understood.* "

Jeff's self-centeredness, his lack of personal discipline, and the gruff controlling tone that he used at home were taught to him indirectly by his raging, uncontrollable, cruel father. The great missing element of love and sacrifice for others was never shown, and thus never understood by my friend. Even when Christ entered his soul at age 25, he battled an uneasy feeling of unworthiness. So, it was next to impossible for this emotionally unprepared dad to build fulfilling relationships and to establish kindness and honesty in that home. As a result, his four growing teens became self-centered; and they had to learn how to handle life's hard knocks through the bad advice of unsaved people outside their home. Without occasional altering suggestions from Spirit-led friends, this entire family would have been lost to the calloused world and eaten up by Satan's wicked workings. The third-generation adults have allowed God's Word to alter their bitterness; but still raising a healthy functional family with loving relationships has become very difficult. They did not have a positive model to follow!

PERSONALITY ROLES

In looking to make a difference in families like this that you know, it is helpful to understand the four personality roles children are forced to fill in a dysfunctional family. First, let me define the term that describes a homelife with very little love and no wholesome, healthy characteristics: A Dysfunctional Family is **a household where harmony between the members is lost, and relationships are distant, critical, disturbing (even dangerous), with no change in sight.**

When the children are not supported or understood, and their feelings are not considered of any value, the offspring in this type of home develop one of four main characteristics in trying to navigate the conflicts that arise. Jeff's four children became exactly what the psychology professors and licensed family counselors describe in these transforming roles.

In my last pastorate in an impoverished Pennsylvania suburb, I found several families who portrayed these four qualities. In working with one man to help him come out of the street drug culture, he told me he and his three younger brothers illustrated the four traits perfectly. As I was counseling him and his girlfriend over a severe relational problem, John told me that he had been the one who tried to protect everyone in his troubled house. The second sibling always joked around to reduce the tension, the third was a loner and afraid of everything, and the youngest was the hero who excelled outside the home. He left at an early age to get away from the constant sadness and negativity.

Scapegoat, mascot, loner, and **hero** are the roles children learn to play to get through the brokenness.[1] That is exactly what my Jeff & Susan (fictional names) created with their four children.

1. First, the only daughter lived as the **Scapegoat,** the one who took most of the scorn and ridicule from others in the family. She always believed her dad would change, especially after they started going to church together. She became the emotionally healthier one with a positive outlook. This also meant pointing out the issues and trying to solve the quarrels and mistreatment. But soon, the rest of her siblings resented her, thinking she always claimed to know best - they refused to cooperate. The authoritative dad often became upset with her trying to fix things or change his way of operating. He

---

[1] Jimmie Ray Lee & Dan Strickland, *Living Free Participant's Guide,* Turning Point Ministries Chattanooga, TN, 1999, 33.

robustly blamed any family drama on her, again unwilling to take any responsibility himself. These responses pushed Cara away from the others, and gradually to rebel, act out, and draw attention to herself. That caused the opposite of what she had intended—more chaos in the family and more anger from her demanding dad.

She has since found strength in her Lord and a good, caring husband. She has the courage to scold and discipline her children, and she was able to take good care of her aging, widowed father. This worn-out man now depends much on his mature, forgiving, and God-fearing daughter.

2. The **Mascot**. The oldest son, like his father, never learned how to be open and honest with others. His life was often just a façade, never showing the real Tom. There was no trust in the anger-ridden and self-centered house he was raised in. As a result, it was very hard for him to share his personal thoughts and ambitions, even with his own wife. Unlike his dad, he was wiser and more determined to do things better and to provide for his daughter what she needed to become a responsible adult. However genetically, he did have a temper that flared when wife or work or neighbor got in his way.

Now as a child, Tom was the mascot or house clown. Joking and getting others to laugh would often take the tension away. He would draw everyone's attention, and the rest of the family would favor him when decisions needed to be made. Even now in his forties, this man with a sanguine (easy going) personality still tries to look at things with a positive and humorous viewpoint. Like a good salesman he will try to swing people his way. Yet occasionally disappointment will make him become irate with people.

3. The third child became the **Loner**. This boy was usually afraid of his father. He avoided encounters with Pop, and spent much time to himself, daydreaming about how he wished things could be. He would leave the room when arguments arose, play by himself, and not feel a part of the family. As a teen, this lost child found different kinds of friends, got involved in drugs, and even now stays away from happy family events like birthdays and holidays. There was little love between him and his two brothers, and neither parent would fairly nor tenderly discipline them. However, his adult sister is still trying to love this lost brother (Roy) into stability.

4. Then there was the **Hero**. The fourth child, also a son, exited the house early to make his own life. He had tried in his positive, outgoing personality to help his siblings get out of their trap. But being the youngest, his suggestions about fairness or standing up to Dad's meanness, were never taken seriously. He was teased by his older brothers, babied by mom, and criticized by his hypocritical dad, so he became successful outside the home. He did well in sports and with his grades. Jake made money with his determined nature and friendly, persuasive attitude, enabling him to accomplish much and make a lot more cash as a young adult. However, he was never able to fully heal from the hurt.

   Jake's life goal was to show his father that he would rise above poverty and loss of significance and achieve much more than anyone else in the family. With his good job, he was able to relish in his hobby of fixing old farm tractors, which was something his father also enjoyed doing but seldom had the cash to accomplish. With his shrewd ability to buy and sell cars at a profit, Jake made a small fortune. He was more than willing to brag about it and to give gifts to his siblings to verify his accomplishments. Perhaps he was hoping money would buy a better relationship with his brothers and sister, and maybe his nephews and nieces. But the younger, successful uncle soon found his generosity would generate only bitterness, envy, and unkind gossip.

We will learn more about these four personality traits in future chapters. For instance, in chapter 7, I will seek to show the difference agape love can make in the way each young adult of a chaotic home can begin to express sacrificial caring for their own children, no matter their personality. And in Chapter 8 we will look at how each trait can handle the need to forgive a parent. In addition, when we discuss overcoming bad habits and disturbing strongholds in chapter 9, we will differentiate how certain personalities handle disappointment and neglect in a variety of ways.

IMPORTANT CONSIDERATIONS

But now consider two important points gleaned from the disorder of the overly ruled family. Where there is a "Controlling Parent," two overwhelming principles will be very noticeable:

1. Dysfunction is generational. There is a continual passing on of practices and postures in distorted families from one generation to another. The grandfather of Jeff's family was addicted to alcohol and abused his family in the 1950s was the start of the problem. He was not only hard to live with, but at an early age he had decided to reject God from his life. Money and alcohol were his idols. Both

> *"This lifestyle will carry on from generation to generation until the Lord is invited to arrest the process."*

issues work against the mind to ruin kindness and reasoning, and then in a demonic way destroy the many other lives that person is responsible to raise and guide into the future. This man fell hard after the first temptation mentioned in 1 John 2:16, "craving for physical pleasure," (NLT) which we will discuss more fully in chapter 3.

A pattern of immoral living and disdain for his Creator established an environment that caused the three previously innocent children (including Jeff's older brother and sister) to live out and pass on the attitudes and habits of their angry parents. This lifestyle and mindset will carry on from generation to generation until the Lord is invited to arrest this degenerating process.

My friend Jeff never learned how to trust people in the home or outside of it. He was not informed as a child or teen that God cared about his life and his soul. So, the way to deal with children became the way his callous father did it—let his wife handle them and he would yell so they all were afraid of him when he came home. This second-generation dad (a new term I want to use is 'Perpetuator') unknowingly planted the seeds for more undisciplined selfishness, unkind deeds and words, and real doubt of significance, leaving no room for godly love or value in life. So, his children, the third generation (I will call them 'Inheritors'), did not know how to handle disappointment or solve sibling squabbles, making them also ill-equipped to parent well.

To prove their own worth, Jeff's sons and daughter copied their father's self-centeredness, pride, lack of morals, and anger. These negative traits and parts of personalities were nurtured in a dysfunctional home because love was not taught nor demonstrated, manners and respect were never shown, and guidance to develop talents and gifts from God was not provided. Currently the fourth generation of this troubled family is vexed with the difficulty of dealing with the same misinformation and misunderstanding!

2. Influence of a Controlling Personality causes long-term damage. A family leader with a strong authoritative personality is probably the most devastating factor in bringing about family disunity. This selfish adult will not only deprive his/her children of needs and certainly wants; but will often abuse them verbally, emotionally, physically, and/or sexually. I suggest these vile actions bring trauma that will greatly affect how the children begin to feel about themselves. And then this injurious parent severely damages how the offspring behaves and relates to others when older.

As a result, no one in the family is stable. The psychological impact is usually extreme, bringing about future fear and depression. Twenty percent of all teens in America were suffering with severe depression at the end of 2019.[2] This carries into the adult life of the abused until professional or biblical help is accepted and followed.

---

[2] National Institute of Mental Health Report, Depression Overview, nimh.nih.gov., June 1, 2022

We can better understand now the frightening statement of Jehovah God in Deuteronomy 5 regarding the second of the Ten Commandments to make no idol for yourself to worship. When a father sinfully refuses to care for the needs of anyone but himself, he is idolizing himself and crafting others who will act the same way. Such a dysfunctional family cycle is the fulfillment of this biblical curse, "For I, the Lord God, will punish the children for the sin of the fathers to the third and fourth generation of those who hate Me" (Deuteronomy 5:9 NIV). I see this as not only God's punishment on one man's sin, but that the controlling father or mother makes a negative, lasting influence on all the offspring.

Let us look at how the judgment on the parent works in the family. When the Controlling Dad (as in my opening story) lifts himself high above the rest and takes away the self-worth or personal value of the child and mate, he sets up a situation where he not only sins more, but he keeps his offspring from loving him at the time and for years in the future. His foolish pride pushes his kids away. He then suffers the consequence of reaping what he sows. In turn, he grows to hate people and God more as his miserable life continues. It appears that Jehovah God brings punishment on this kind of demonic dad.

Jeff's father became extremely belligerent and snarly as he suffered with health problems in his late fifties. Few family members cared to talk with this dissenting and disorderly man. Jeff once asked me to visit his dad in the hospital where he loudly and profoundly cursed and swore at me, demanded that I leave, and screamed to the nurse to get this preacher out of there. Although this real-life illustration fits my premise, I believe there are other countless examples in America where the hateful parent suffers in the future for his idolatry.

A loud, bossy man or woman is usually a meet-my-needs-first person. He or she will establish an atmosphere of self-love that will become engrained in the minds of their children all through their impressionable years and far into adulthood. Therefore, the young ones will most often unknowingly repeat the bad habits and cruel actions that caused their own misery. These foolish mistakes or evil deeds do come naturally, but the decisions they make daily and the preferences follow are their own, yet they most often become just like the ways of Controlling Dad. Thus these individual sinful actions bring the Lord's wrath on the troubled pre-teen, or the revolting teenager. This is because they refuse to acknowledge or comprehend their own intentional sin, and then will not repent of it.[3]

This principle of punishing the children is not just because God is jealous and promises deserved retribution, but also because the victims decide to remain victims and usually do not try to alter their behavior. (See chapter 9). Because we are all born with a strong sin nature, odds are set that the acts of the curse will become the second generation's choice. Children will not have interest in sharing toys, speaking pleasantly, putting others above themselves, figuring out what is right or wrong, fair or not, obeying the other parent, or listening to what others say a loving God can do for them. So, they reap what they sow with their incorrect and self-centered thinking and doing. Galatians 6:8 describes this so well, "Those who plant (or live) only to satisfy their own sinful nature will harvest decay and death from that sinful nature" (NLT). *The child might not recognize the role he or she plays in this cosmic principle. Here the Counselor/Pastor must help!*

---

[3] Interview with Dr. David Van Dyke, Wheaton College, Wheaton, IL, September 2020.

It is possible, of course, that curious or extra intelligent children might notice most of their friends do not have such a difficult, unfair family life. When these somewhat enlightened persons ask questions or plead for change, often the cruel parent will clamp down harder on them to continue their sinful control, screaming at and striking them more frequently, or even threatening to kill another family member.

Only an outside Christian influence can save the day for the child who longs for something better. In my experience, it will either be the scapegoat (fixer) or hero (independent one) who takes the chance to listen to a whole different paradigm of life. The gospel then will not only open their mind to better things but will also pull on their heart to believe it is possible for them to overcome the trap. These two personalities, wanting the most to leave the snare of   disorder, will be open to a solid plan that sets them free from the cruel emotional tentacles that squeeze them. They may be able to comprehend that their spiritually lost and blinding environment is where they need not (must not) stay.

When the Holy Spirit gets hold of this searching soul, HE will show them that God has a freeing plan for their life. With the encouragement of a Christian friend, they will begin to understand they, like everyone else, are a sinner; and a Savior has been provided for them to get to know personally. As Jesus draws them (John 6:44, 65), they will be overwhelmed with the love of their Christian acquaintance. They will

" *Shown their value as a person and realize...what they thought was never possible.* "

most often overcome their fear and be ready to jump into a rewarding life where they are shown their value as a person and realize they can experience what they thought was never possible. Then this saved young person can be discipled and nurtured and taught the answers for a loving, powerful abundant life (John 10:10). As other godly people help with the revived individual of a broken family, he or she is often able to stop and then reverse course. Along with peace in their hungry heart, they will find inner strength to stand against the onslaught of Satan. One way or another, God will use other people to help this wounded but healing person to live powerfully among the carnage of dysfunction. Or He will open a way of escape through staying with other family members or Christian friends.

When my troubled friend Jeff got saved, he felt the difference of freedom in his soul, but he was not ready to translate that into becoming a better parent. Because of the Deuteronomy 5:9 Principle, he was not able or not willing to fully submit to God and allow Him to help conquer the temptations to give in to the worldly life. Although he was saved, he was never desirous of giving his Lord control of his decisions or ambitions in life. He would usually not let go of the tendency that made his mind say, "I am boss! I will control my house and my future! I will do it my way!" I watched the spiritual battle wage ferociously inside Jeff's mind. The great struggle of deciding to be sold out for God took too many years with small steps forward, and big steps backward.

Other people in similar situations can or have overcome the curse sooner. *I believe the help I give in this book will allow counselors to bring change more effectively for good. Plus, this material should encourage more sincere submission to God and HIS Word.* There is definitely power from God to cause minds, attitudes, and reactions to improve in a dysfunctional family. *And you who are reading this can build the kind of stability and strength needed to alter many lives of troubled children and young adults.*

After Jeff's wife became gravely sick and he also developed some difficult health problems, he realized it was past time to get serious with living out his faith. Praise God, in his late fifties, Jeff finally became a true follower of Jesus Christ and worshiped and witnessed for Him very effectively. Unfortunately, his four grown children by then had taken his same earlier attitude of calling on God only when troubles came. As expected, their own children, the inheritors, all suffered with the serious pain and penalty of dysfunction.

The curse is very strong. It is up to a counselor or strong Christian friend to guide them to victory over it. *Therefore, I am challenging you, the reader, with the principles and Scriptures in this book!*

Chapter 2

WHOSE FAULT IS IT?

Now that we have looked at the ugliness of the Dysfunctional Family from one perspective, I must point out other ways in which God's well-designed early human institution is being brought down. It is not only the strongly authoritative parent that causes chaos by ignoring the conflicts and squabbles of the children or in refusing to encourage or compliment the ideas and wishes of their offspring.

Christian author June Hunt first came up with the four kinds of parents who cause dysfunctional families in *Making Peace with Your Past*.[4] The **Controlling Parent** was Jeff's father who forced the children to comply. There is also the **Conforming Parent** who has rules and regulations for the family and manipulates people to follow them. Third is the **Coddling Parent** who is very lenient and spoils the kids.

---

[4] June Hunt, *Dysfunctional Families - Making Peace with Your Past*, Aspire Press, a division of Rose Publishing, Torrance, CA, 2014, 35-36.

Finally, the **Chaotic Parent** is the laid-back one who does not guide, but lets things happen by chance.

I want to expand now on these four types of flawed parents by developing their personalities and showing how their individual weaknesses hurt their own children. This will come from my 46 years of pastoral experience and hundreds of family counseling cases. Let me start at the beginning with the very first family and their big relational problems.

ADAM'S FAMILY

When the Creator said in the beginning that man should not be alone, He provided the woman to be Adam's "help meet "(Genesis 2:18, (KJV)); "helper suitable for him" (NIV.) That was the first family; and Satan has sought to attack it ever since. The tempter first damaged the relationship between the couple, causing doubt, self-will, and lack of trust among them. This would boil over and burn families from then on. Because of their first sin of pride and desire to become wiser, their firstborn son was destined to be tormented with choices that would fulfill his own gratification but would never benefit the rest of his four-person family.

As I study the story of Adam's family, I can see how the original perfect family quickly became dysfunctional because of sin. It appears, for example, that Adam's personality was more passive and laid-back. "(Eve) gave some to her husband who was with her" (Genesis 3:6). This verse implies that he allowed her to go forward, then he copied her aggressive move. Eve quickly became the dominant one. "For Adam was formed first, then Eve. And Adam was not the one deceived, it was the woman who was deceived and became a sinner" (1 Timothy 2:13-14).

Even though they were both forgiven by their Lord, they evidently did not set the best example for their two boys in the following years. Cain wanted things his way, not God's. Apparently the first dad neither saw nor countered his son's brewing anger. Adam did not help Cain understand the Heavenly Father's rule for a sacrificial lamb at worship time. Rather the young farmer offered the best of the crops he produced with his own strength for the mysterious Master whom he could not hear nor see.

Adam's sin nature, I believe, developed in a way that he did not become a good head of the home. The first human father was unable to coach his strong-willed and determined son. Perhaps Cain's ambitions and drives were too difficult for Adam to work with. Adam was not a confident leader; he was more defensive, slow to react, and willing to shirk responsibility. "The woman You put here ...she gave me ..." (Genesis. 3:12). Adam allowed the first family to quickly become dysfunctional as he was a Chaotic Dad (see definition in paragraph two above).

While we are in Genesis, let us look more closely at Cain before we get back to the four flawed parents. With Adam allowing for family issues to continue to occur, it is no wonder there was sibling rivalry in the first household. Cain can be viewed as a choleric (quick tempered) personality, aggressive, setting his own reasoned rules, even a hero character (one of the four described in chapter 1) that went wrong. It could be surmised that Cain could not master his jealousy (Genesis 4:6-7) and was rebellious toward God as well as his own weaker earthly father. The Bible does not explain all that happened in Genesis 4. Yet, the Apostle John does talk about Cain as a murderer and that as a child his "actions were evil, but Abel's deeds were righteous" (1 John 3:12). Imagine the loud fights the two boys had. Where was Dad's discipline? My imagination pictures Adam as very proud of his firstborn and happy to teach him how to toil in the ground. Eve probably favored the second, softer, compliant, and obedient child, similar to Isaac and Rebecca's poor parenting of Esau and Jacob (Genesis 25:27-28). The more laid-back uninvolved male of the house often leaves the guiding of the kids to the more alert and aggressive female. This type of mom naturally does not draw out the proper respect from a dominant son, and Chaotic Dad does not fill in.

FOUR WAYS IT STARTS WITH DAD AND MOM

Let us move on to the other types of parents that create dysfunction in their households. A quick reminder of the poor family dynamics in the house of the authoritative parent is as follows:

1. The **Controlling** Parent. When a controlling adult is selfish and demanding, the harmony and cooperation a family should have is off balance. Everyone must adjust to the wishes of a very grumpy dad or an over-complaining mom. The submissive mate is usually nervous, and the children never know what to expect. With the youngsters there is little comfort or security, and they may constantly fear they will be screamed at or struck for just being in the grouch's way.

   There are few attempts by the subjugated mate to protect or aid the weaker members of the family. Usually there are no set plans or methods for everyone to work together on anything. Nor do they feel comfortable enough to offer an opinion about what goes on behind the home's closed doors. Looking outside for help is taboo.

The controlling parent wants no one else to know of unhappy times at home.

Years of being denied or put down bring a sense of not mattering to others. When the child reaches grade school, he or she notices that many kids they know don't live in fear or obscurity at their house. The wounded child wonders what is wrong with him or why the alcoholic father doesn't appreciate him. Or the emotionally unstable, demanding mother never asks how her daughter feels about things, nor does she try to care for her when the youngster is sick. The child's wishes are never met. The children are never asked personal questions about what they would like to do on the weekend or what they are working on in school.

2. The **Conforming** Parent insists on everyone doing things the same way, the right way. The leading adult is possessive as well as demanding. He or she goes overboard with pressure on the children so dad and mom can feel good about themselves. Conforming parents have lost the idea of what they wanted to accomplish with the family other than that things must run smoothly. As a result, they use manipulation, persuasion, or even trickery to keep everyone in line. Any new ideas of how things could be done differently are dismissed. Mama must have things her way or Father knows best, so don't rock the boat!

    The kids cannot think for themselves or make choices without an argument. Dad may want to live out his childhood again through the son in athletics or good grades. This parent then becomes mentally dependent on the success of an unwilling child, and often situations do not work out as expected. This type of mother will work on the child's emotions by crying in front of the family over the way the child responds or disobeys. If this son or daughter does not turn out right, she claims to blame herself, but she will overly criticize the child to get what she wants.

Conforming Parents will attempt to show their growing children how to meet their parents' needs rather than allowing young minds to accomplish what the child's heart leads them to do. They don't try to discover what is on the minds of their teens. So, kids become lonely, isolated, or frustrated and often do foolish things with their own bodies such as cutting, suffering from bulimia, or taking drugs.

As a result, the children usually choose one of two different paths. They will either become very reliant on their parents making their decisions for them, or conversely, will turn inwardly rebellious. Children with the first temperament (too submissive) will have trouble growing up and doing things for themselves in a job or career. Children with separation thoughts will make secret plans to deliberately disappoint a meticulous adult or maybe even to run away and live in the streets to be free from their family slavedriver. Independent-minded children raised by a conforming adult will usually maintain a rebellious streak as they grow up. Life will be centered around making themselves happy, ignoring reason or logic, and lacking love for others. Such children will also not yield to authority when they become adults.

3. The **Coddling** Parent. This person is the exact opposite of the conforming parent. Here, children are the center of attention to an extreme and everything is done to favor and patronize them. The youngsters' feelings are usually protected, priorities are scheduled

as they wish, and disagreements are avoided at all costs. However, dad or mom have little authority. Really, they do not want it; rather, they deal with whatever comes up in a kind of free-wheeling manner. Consequently, these kids are also undisciplined and unprepared to become adults.

A strong-willed child here will run the home with little correction. The shy or easy-going child will feel confused and find it difficult to build up self-esteem or seek to accomplish much. They are not taught limitations, boundaries, personal value, and how to work hard toward achievement. In fact, the coddling parents feel they should never force their children to do anything. Their philosophy is: "just suit yourself, dear; make your own decisions, and full happiness should be experienced in our whole house."

But the spoiled children will make childish choices. The adults excuse their mistakes and try to cover for them, so the kids never feel any consequences for their selfish behavior or sibling squabbles. The parents are good at finding others to blame: the coach, the teacher, or another parent. When trials come or plans are not fulfilled, the children have not learned to deal with disappointment. As a result, sinful displays of uncontrolled emotions or serious experiences of jealousy or greed stay with them until adulthood. Because they were never taught to feel responsible or to deal with life's unfair situations their immaturity will likely cause them to be egotistical, dysfunctional parents themselves later in life.

4. The **Chaotic** Parent is lackadaisical and disorganized, and never had much discipline or instruction to achieve anything special in growing up. So, as parents now, they lack motivation and ambition

and have no desire to help their children work for good grades or pursue music or athletics. It could be that dad is too busy at work, watching TV, or playing video games to really get involved with his kids. Perhaps mom was spoiled by grandma and never learned to fold clothes or cook special meals or even keep her own bedroom tidy.

As a result, the chaotic house of this second generation is usually a mess. Everyone must do their own laundry and buy their own clothes, while mom watches too many soap operas or goes back to bed after kids go to school. She may have to take depression medicine or just wash down her cares with a bottle. Her guilt for not raising her children right has probably weighed on her too long, especially if a son or daughter has rebelled. The children might have begun to fight with their parents over things they want and cannot get because they say, "Mother doesn't work either outside or inside the home" or Father's job doesn't bring in enough income to keep up with the Jones'. The unengaged Chaotic Parent not only promotes disorder and jealousy but will open the home to great danger. Trouble is sure to come either in the era of teenagers or when they become out-of-control young adults.

A TRAGIC EXAMPLE

My wife Bettie and I, along with a few others from our church, witnessed a tragic, life-changing example of a Coddling parent. Sherry was a good mother who cared deeply for her two daughters but often had no resources to provide food for them. She came to us one spring in desperate need of food and clothing. She told us she had escaped from a mean boyfriend in the big city about 70 miles away. She had moved to our small suburb to rebuild her relationship with her ex-husband in hopes that he had changed from his drug habit and would provide for their children this time. After living together for two weeks, she discovered that it was not working out.

We supplied them with nutritional food from our church's food pantry, provided school supplies, and encouraged them to come to our church and youth ministry. We discovered that the oldest daughter had some emotional problems with the older men in her mom's life. She wanted to stay in her room and not go to school. Despite her mother's attempts, Leslie would not leave the house. So, Sherry gave in with much sympathy and a coddling parent personality. She spoiled her oldest daughter and did not get outside help or counsel.

Sherry's younger teenager had the opposite personality. She enjoyed school, made friends easily, and was outgoing even at church. Sammie's social lifestyle made other demands on her mom including community activities with no vehicle for transportation and school expenses with no parental income. Sammie was involved in escapades without telling her mother where she was going and when she would come home. Despite our advice to be more rigid and disciplined with her daughters, Sherry could not bring herself to put restrictions on them nor to corral their selfish conduct. Dad was not home most of the time, and when he was, he was mean and grouchy under the influence of a chemical substance.

My wife counseled Sherry and did a discipleship program with her over a few months. She accepted Christ as Savior and was progressing well with a changed heart and genuine desire to live the way Jesus wanted her to. A district school psychologist got involved to help Leslie with her fear of school. Our small church did what we could and aided them quite a bit with utility bills and attempts at making friends with the extra shy daughter.

At Christmas time several ladies bought nice gifts for the three females. Others from church provided some nice basic holiday decorations in their house. We had an exciting Christmas Eve program at the church with these three and everyone else feeling the warmth of the season and love for one another. It was not until the next afternoon that I discovered the horror that Sherry's family had experienced the night before.

Dad returned home late and passed out on the living room floor with the frightening scene of overdose shock. Sherry performed CPR and they called 911. When paramedics and police arrived and loaded him into the ambulance, an officer ran a scan on Sherry's history and found she was wanted by the authorities for an earlier truancy misdemeanor in their previous city. They handcuffed her in front of her screaming kids and took her to jail on Christmas Eve. What a chaotic frightening experience to ruin an otherwise heart-warming special day!

Because of Sherry's leniency and inaction, the help she thought she was giving to her unruly daughters all came to poison their present situation. The shock of her being away for three months, one daughter staying with an unproductive Dad, and the younger going to live with a more positive grandparent left everyone confused and bitter. Eventually Mom and the girls were reunited, and they moved to another city where they struggled all over again with trust and support.

At least for the present, Satan has succeeded in ruining the seed planted, and the spiritual progress we had made with the family came to a halt. Currently, this dysfunctional family is scattered, and the kids are not doing well. There was a great lack of discipline to overcome; yet we were sure that Mom is a believer. We hope and pray that her daughters will be influenced by other godly people in the future and be able to overcome the atmosphere of the drastically broken home of their past. Oh, if only there could have been a much happier ending! And we pray as in Isaiah 55:11, Lord, may your Word as You promised, still accomplish its purpose as You sent it to that precious family.

In summary, these four weaker styles of troubled leaders of the home have yielded to the temptations and bad habits of earthly wisdom, selfish ambition, or great disorder. When we see these evil characteristics showing up in a family, we should ask God for open opportunities to help and the right words to say!

We will learn next about the sneaky temptations that haunt "flawed parents."

Chapter 3

SATAN DESTROYS THE GOODNESS IN FAMILIES

The Bible tells us in Genesis 3 that God allowed Satan to tempt Eve in the Garden, and the first woman yielded. Romans 5 explains that because of Adam's determination to follow Eve and disobey God's command, all of us sin and are prone to selfishness. As a result, we were all born with the curiosity and capacity to want to be great and powerful like God and to control our own lives. The devil's words in this very first temptation incident were, "For God knows that when you eat from it your eyes will be opened, and you will be like God, knowing good and evil" (Genesis 3:5). Thus, according to Romans 5, the sin nature born into us shows that when Adam and Eve fell in sin, all their future descendants became capable of falling to many different temptations, seeking to identify "good and evil" but unable to discern the difference.

"GOOD AND EVIL"

As we learned in chapter 1, some individuals take this idolatry (worshiping ourselves or things as gods) to extremes. The things people living in sin reach for involve either pleasure, possessions, or power. Satan still uses these three prime temptations to keep people out of God's true heavenly family. Or, in the same way, to distract believers so they will not further God's Kingdom. These tools of the devil are specifically mentioned in 1 John 2:15-17: the cravings of sinful man, the lust of his eyes, and the boasting of what he has and does.

To say it another way, all people will be bothered by one of three temptations that try to take control of them. The first possible area of life to be tested could be meeting bodily needs in excess through means such as food, drugs, sex, alcohol, smokes, skin lotions, or even too much exercise. This enticement pulls on the natural man to satisfy cravings that come from our human make up. Many Christians who may be weak in faith can fall for this temptation also. The King James Bible calls it the "lust of the flesh."

Second, our minds can lust for or desire many material things that we think will satisfy, such as houses, cars, tools, pools, gadgets, electronics, or just plain luxury. These things have a powerful tendency to draw both Christians and non-Christians in the direction of selfishness or greed.

Then the third area folks pursue is popularity and praise. Many people want to make something of themselves so they will be admired and remembered as someone important or above the rest. Troubling areas for this temptation include education, position, politics, physical ability, or achievement--anything to become popular so they will be lifted

> "*To control our own lives and destinies without God is to know good and evil.*"

up in others' eyes. To control our own lives and to seek to master our own destinies without God is to know good and to know evil. We experiment with and discover new ideas and better opportunities to build our pride and to selfishly increase our worth.

Now these personal achievements or goals in themselves are not wrong! In fact, they may be used to develop much good in the world. But it turns evil when we fail to keep negative and positive decisions in proper balance. To purposefully run our lives our self-centered way instead of allowing integrity and honesty to guide us, is to invite Satan and sin to rule our minds and souls. That is always a wrong decision. Such a person will too often be open to sinful temptations and be led to reject the Creator's better plan for them.

It is fine to have dreams, goals, and big plans. But when they consume a person's time and attention and become all he or she lives for to the detriment of spouse and children, those attractions or items or rewards become, as the Bible puts it, loving the world and the things in it. Then there is little room to exercise love for people, the real purpose for which we were designed. So, if the love of the Father is not in us (1 John 2:15), we cannot properly love the people whom God has miraculously and purposefully placed in our care, our physical family.

THE DEVIL ATTACKING THE FAMILY BOND

I have discovered that a parent caught in one of these areas of worldliness will often choose that temptation over his/her offspring. Counselors hear countless sorrowful testimonies of mothers who choose drugs over their own kids, or of children having watched greedy dads choose more wealth over care for their moms. The cold hard facts are that when an adult is captured by these allurements, they are headed for dysfunction in life. Where then is the goodness, kindness, and love God designed for the family?

The next generation will suffer from lack of care and concern because the devil has worked in the parents' snared mind via pleasure, possessions, or power. As a result, in time, one or more of their kids will often fall for that same temptation as they try to grow up and contemplate what is important in their lives. (See chapter 1, page 22 "Dysfunction Is Generational.")

We need supernatural help and wisdom to experience the abundant life God intended. Satan, the Thief, tries to steal God's family blessings. (John 10:10), with the temptations that he throws against all families.

His goal is to destroy the place where good relationships and godly traits are to be established as patterns of God's love. Unfortunately, because of the Fall, each of us has a strong tendency to satisfy ourselves first. That's the power of sin and ego that each man, woman, and child faces. Yet, it's only after a person becomes a believer in Christ that he or she can succeed in fighting against the draw of those strong enticements.

The personality we are born with, and our home environment have much to do with how we allow fleshly appeals to control us. We need to understand that the four types of flawed parenting addressed in

> *"His goal is to destroy the place where good relationships and godly traits are established."*

chapter 2 were influenced by the negative environment they grew up in. But they are also greatly influenced later by the same three temptations that Satan successfully brought against Adam and Eve in the first beautiful Garden of Eden; and then later tried to use against Jesus in the wilderness, without success. The devil knows how to work on personalities to expand the sin nature and eradicate families.

TWO AGGRESSIVELY FLAWED PARENTS

For instance, the **Controlling** Father may relish the power that his loud voice or demanding words portray. And when the wife or children are afraid or overly compliant, that satisfies his craving to be on top and to have others bowing to him. This is idolatry because he (or the mother) subconsciously wants to be like a god to the rest of the family. As stated before, this leader of the home is far more concerned about his or her needs and wishes than the wants, likes, interests, or needs of spouse or kids. This authoritative person finds fault and criticizes everyone else, proudly building himself up. There is little thought of loving the others he's responsible for. Instead, his deep feelings and fondness are for himself because he has been captured by that third temptation to love himself too much. (See reference to idolatry in chapter 1). To seek to gain overwhelming power in his house is this man's main sin.

Then remember, **Conforming** Mothers or Fathers need specific order at home to give them inner peace. She or he will carefully accumulate many things and work hard to keep items in a systematic way or in a specific place. The father will also train subjugated mom and all the kids to know where the toys and tools are, to make sure they use them the right way, and to put them back in the right place. Their struggles are not only the temptation for many gadgets, but the sin to possess their children.

In a way, the Controlling and Conforming adults are of very similar makeup. They are both authoritative, claim to be wiser than the rest, and expect respect and submission. The demanding one gets control by a raised voice or harsh words, where the calmer Conforming parent will dominate others by manipulating moods or buying cooperation. Since these family leaders really believe that God (or fate) has put them in charge of everyone else, they cannot feel good about their lives until all are following through with their well thought-out (nearly perfectionistic) methods of operation.

The Conforming Mother, for example, without realizing it will often become the guide, protector, and decision-maker for her precious little chicks. She easily becomes like a "mini god" and oversteps boundaries (see chapter 6). It is another form of idolatry that will stifle

> " *Happiness depends on how well she's lived out her life through her children.* "

the maturity of her brood. She feels she is extremely important to her children; but the secret truth is they are now extremely important to her. Mom's life begins to wrap around them so much that when the time comes, her offspring just must "turn out right." So, she becomes codependent on them. Her kids have become more important than dad or anything else that might be happening around the family. This managing parent's self-worth and future happiness depends on how well she's lived out her life through her children. Slip up or failure is not an option.

But as the kids grow older, some teens comply and live for their mother even as adults. But others rebel and argue about the freedom they never had because of her possessiveness. Both mom and these children live unhappily and mistrusting for a long time. Manipulating people our way for our benefit is nearly always wrong. Exceptions might be when a child cannot physically take care of him/herself, a parent is expected and even required to do many things for them. In such cases the children are helped and encouraged in their attempts to do life slowly and carefully. But even then, mom or dad could do harm if they care for these special needs in a selfish way.

This Conforming Parent is basically conceited and is full of boastfulness or selfish ambition. To purposefully mold a child into being what they want him or her to be is not only egotistical, but it can also lead to the more serious diabolical act of trying to master their future. The devil constantly tries to work a controlling power grab in nearly every person from birth to death, especially the unsaved. He puts self-centered thoughts in the Conforming mind, like: "Look to your own rights! Your way is the best way. With all your sacrificing - you deserve their obedience."

Satan even sought to entice Jesus into being selfish or obtaining his own self-glory in an amazing crowd-pleasing way. Remember Matthew 4:5-7 where he took Him to the holy city and had him stand on the highest point of the temple. His suggestion was that Jesus jump from a very high pinnacle so people below could see a miracle of angels protecting Him (or gravity being defied in some invisible, miraculous way). The devil thought that this would have caused Jesus to pridefully get praise for Himself. Satan foolishly thought he could get Christ to force His Father's hand, and to do what the Son seemingly wanted rather than God's divine plan of humility and full obedience to His serious mission. However, this would have been a selfish sin on Jesus' part, something the perfect righteous God-man could never do. Yet in this text Jesus gives us an example that we can follow to resist temptation. He knew He did not come to earth to fulfill His own wishes, but to do the will of God who sent Him (John 6:38). The Son of God would not be tricked into self-gratification but would always accomplish things for His Father's honor.

As the children of God mature, they should discover and accept their purpose in life. I believe this is to continually find ways to honor their heavenly Father. "Glorify the Lord with me, let us exalt his name together" (Psalm 34:3). For the believer, life is not about pleasing self but rather about pleasing our Creator and lifting up those around us for their benefit. We are not to worship any other god including ourselves as that too is idolatry. Our praise and honor are to go only to our amazing Savior.

Let me share with you some examples of the damage that Conforming Parents can do. In the years I spent in my last church in a neglected suburb, I saw many families that were struggling with the drug addiction of their teens and young adults. In counseling with distraught parents, I often heard, "I tried so hard to keep my kid away from this problem. I would talk with him kindly, plead with her emotionally, threaten him strongly, get outsiders to warn or scare her of the consequences, but nothing worked. They did it anyway."

As I would delve into the family history and sympathetically ask questions, quite often I found that Mom or Dad was either overprotective or too forceful about how the child lived. So, the response of their children was a quest for independence or a plan to foil the parents' rules or demands. This mentality would often push them into the wrong crowd or risky behavior. And Mom would cry, "What did we do wrong?" Dad would ask, "Why did this happen to us?"

The Conforming adult leader of the house should be honoring boundaries (more in chapters 6 and 9) of the son or daughter who is trying to discover who they are and what they should be in life. Forcing or persuading a pre-conceived way upon the young person will usually bring resistance and develop mistrust. It is better to make loving suggestions, to earnestly get their opinions, and to encourage the children, giving them chances to find what best fits their own personality and desires, rather than to just do what their peers say.

If the authoritative parent can be shown to hold back his or her instincts and become one who compliments and supports, the home will be more peaceful, the teen will become more settled, and the parent will find more confidence. Prayerfully trusting the Lord to mold the young person's mind is much more effective than trying to force the parent's will on the youngster. Without this understanding, the Conforming Dad falls into the temptation of pride and yields to the sin of insisting on things that please him, rather than seeking to please his Lord.

TEMPTATION FOR THE MORE SUBJECTIVE "FLAWED PARENTS"

We need to look more closely at the other two failing parents that psychologists describe. The Coddling and Chaotic adults are both from a similar mold.

The Coddling Parent is a person with a melancholy or phlegmatic personality who may make sure the days are managed with the children in mind. Their precious offspring are the center of attention, so whatever toy or electronic gadget is asked for, they will have it in their hands shortly. These folks not only worship their children but believe God expects them to sacrifice for the happiness of the youngsters. In itself, focusing much on them is not wrong. It is seeking to find out what our kids' real interests are and how we can treat them with extra kindness and give helpful gifts at appropriate times. In a later chapter we will discuss that one of the factors in a functional home is to make sure the children feel valued as individuals and are treated as if they are wanted and welcomed as part of a loving unit.

However, a problem arises when these adults become proud of what they are doing and want grandparents and neighbors to notice. Because they desire to be admired by outsiders for their many expensive provisions and great elaborate ideas, they are actually "loving the world" and spoiling the child. They neither see nor care that they are creating envy in the hearts of adult acquaintances or jealousy among their kids' classmates who come over all the time to enjoy the luxuries.

This reminds me of Satan's second temptation for Jesus. He offered the Son of Man a short cut to world power without the suffering or disappointments of life. Jesus would have great sway over people and all the splendor the world could offer if He would just follow and bow to the ruler of the world's treasures. Individuals who use the pleasures of life to buy happiness or seek influence over people to gain popularity are falling into the spiritual trap that the Apostle John warns about in his first letter and that we have referred to above: "Do not love the world or anything in the world. If anyone loves the world, the love of the Father is not in him. . . The world and its desires pass away, but whoever does the will of God lives forever" (I John 2:15, 17).

Worldly Coddling Parents are artfully teaching their children that the love of money and the pride of life are worthy attributes. Secular counselors in the workplace say that such practice causes grown "kids" discontent with future employment, loss of trusted friends, and the shocking absence of quick gratification. These Millennials often blame their dissatisfaction in life on the people who raised them and are no longer there for them. They expect their over-gracious older adults to bail them out or solve their issues or accept their life drama. Finally, if these spoiled younger adults do not want to leave home or decide to come back after messing up their own families, the Coddling Parent becomes depressed or even angry because their children won't grow up or take responsibility.

The Christian counselor needs to find a way to introduce the loving God to the lazy son, the wild daughter, or even the disenchanted grandparents. The softer parents may still be impairing their adult kids and trying with all their might to avoid serious fights, threatened divorce, sudden jail time, or vicious addictions.

These first-generation flawed parents (I call them "Originators") must recognize that their indulgence and leniency were the biggest causes of their kid's longtime immaturity. "Tough love" is the only way to help turn things around. Withholding additional gifts or help until they become grateful and learn to do for themselves often will work. Mom or Dad must also accept the fact of their enabling, for that clearly stunted the social and emotional growth of their second-generation son or daughter.

Such over tolerance has also negatively impacted the third generation (Inheritors) of the family. For they have probably been acting up, wanting more gifts and grace, or have become dull and slothful teenagers. Without good teaching or allowing God to be a vital part of the life of the Grandparents, their easy-going personality that gave the second generation the world and spared the rod has produced sluggish and inactive kids now in their thirties and forties. So, the temptation of materialism made the family dysfunctional, reason and control caused a sinful, demanding lifestyle for the future (third and fourth generations – Deuteronomy 5:9c).

One more wrong parenting style of subjective nature should be addressed briefly. The Chaotic Parent (male or female) has little self-discipline, so things are not done well in the life of the family. Since leading adults live mainly for what feels good or what happens with most ease and little planning, the kids don't have much interest in doing or being anything but what their physical cravings push them to. If not for outside influence from a caring schoolteacher or coach, a Christian teenage friend, or a serious-minded grandparent, there will not be much drive to find their abilities, stretch their minds, do things for others, or achieve more than expected by the parents and siblings.

Confusion reigns in this house because promises are forgotten, schedules are not followed, and needed purchases are made only at the last minute. This failing adult is mentally lazy and unconcerned about the needs of the children. As a result, the offspring are emotionally abandoned and feel unwanted or unnecessary. Their deprivation of love may be temporarily soothed with electronic gadgets and mounds of trendy clothes. The goal here is to keep them quiet and out of the way. Although material things are part of the struggle, the real temptation for this parent is bodily cravings. He or she will depend on sweets each day, lounge around the TV too long, and may have a problem with alcohol. For the Chaotic Parent, satisfying his or her own desires is the priority, overwhelming bodily drives is the enemy's temptation, and selfishness and laziness are the sin-nature that is controlling.

A Chaotic Parent may be found not only in a home with a big paycheck or large bank account. The strong desire to have more can also control the man or woman trying to raise children in poverty. The more dad looks around at bare shelves and broken windows, mother sees crawling insects and overflowing garbage cans, or kids complain about what the neighbors have, the greater the wish for the family to have things that are beyond their means.

We need to remember and even explain that laziness breeds emptiness, emptiness leads to bitterness, and bitterness leads to covetousness.

This unfortunately can lead to theft if the adults don't have the moral bearings that would cause the kids to find ways to be content just a little bit longer. Conversely, a child who has little to eat and only dirty half-broken toys to play with can become sad, lazy, frustrated, and careless also. An envious teen must be aware that stolen goods can quickly become rotten and rusty as well. Young inner city gang members are never taught these principles. Consequently, Chaotic Parents often produce young criminals.

A home like this really needs spiritual help from a mature, caring believer or neighbor. Christians who can bring aid may supply some physical needs personally or through the church. Even more important, Christians can provide love, encouragement, gracious advice, help with the children, insight in dealing with the pain and arguing among family members. Compassionate time spent with the people in this careless house can pay off with great dividends in the future. Soon a hunger for the gospel will rise in the heart of someone in this family. That is a good start in redeeming the Chaotic Parent and some of their victims.

SUMMARY ABOUT FAMILY TEMPTATIONS

Before we close, we must be reminded of Jesus' answer to the temptation of extra bodily pleasures. Satan approached Him after 40 days without food, to turn stones on the ground into loaves of bread to fill His definite hunger. Christ's response to the sure physical craving He had after such a long time of fasting: "Man does not live on bread alone, but on every word that comes from the mouth of God" (Matthew 4:4). Jesus was telling the devil and us that our focus every day needs to be on what our loving Lord can provide in feeding our souls first with His power and peace. Our own physical longings and desires can be set aside. They satisfy only for short periods. But God's cleansing, confidence, and control of life is worth far more than the temporary enjoyment of taste on the tongue or filling of the stomach. That's why our Master said, "Blessed are those who hunger and thirst for righteousness, for they will be filled" (Matthew 5:6).

So, here is the breakdown (as I see it) to what temptations overpower the four Problem Parents, and why their weakness is exploited by the Deceiver. The Controlling Parent is faced over and over with desire for more power over the family. His sin is that he loves himself too much. The Conforming Mother deals with having too many things in order to coax kids to follow her lifestyle. The <u>Coddling</u> Mom will also spoil the family with an abundance of gadgets and goods so she can keep everyone happy superficially. Finally, the <u>Chaotic</u> Dad is far more concerned about how he feels and what he wants than about the supplying of care and value to his wife and distant-feeling children. As you can see, everyone has weak spots to work on, but unfortunately, the flawed parents initially don't wish to admit or overcome their faults. To hunger for righteousness instead of selfishness is not part of their DNA - yet!

So, we pastors and counselors can be used by the Lord to open eyes and encourage moves that would help everyone in the dysfunctional family avoid the devil's temptations and desire a better handle on finding their real potential. Not all will take our advice or allow God to work. Many prefer the easier "broad road leading to destruction" of Matthew 7:13. But I believe it is worth the try to show them the better way. The battle is rough, and the enemy is strong, yet the power of God is so exciting and rewarding to watch and be a part of!

If parents with these types of weaknesses were able to see what they are doing to their families, God's Spirit could bring them to sorrow and repentance. Then much psychological damage to the young ones could be avoided. Remember how George Bailey in the popular Christmas movie, It's A Wonderful Life, was able to see the difference through his guardian angel Clarence. His world and family would be led into the dark side if George gave up and didn't act with integrity and love?

Likewise, a flawed parent could choose to change his or her ways in time to see God protect them from the devil's temptations. It is never too late to repent, restore, and rebuild. The time we spend with the fallen parents and/or injured teens and young adults of our churches allows them to see they need to be looking for a better way to think and react. Our kind guidance in helping them to see the difference can bring them to a place where the Holy Spirit can cause them to want to be restored and convince them that the Word of God will show them how to rebuild their dysfunctional family.

Remember that harmony between the members can be found. Relationships need not be distant, disturbing, or dangerous any longer. (The opposite of my earlier definition of the Dysfunctional family!) God loves His people and has a plan of abundant life for each one to live.

UNIT II

SAVING THE FAMILY

Unit II

SAVING THE FAMILY

Cain had a family; but sinfully lost it! After God took away his opportunity to raise crops from the earth, he decided to raise a city with his own hands, and to live without GOD. As a result, he taught his descendants the same self-centered philosophy. And they by the 5th generation produced the boastful and murderous Lamech. He then raised children to use their God-inborn talents to create idols of bronze, music that dishonored the Lord, and oxen and horses (livestock, Genesis 4:21-22) to selfishly further their power over others.

These ungodly families became very wicked with no regard for one another, and desirous of only control and conquest. Life meant little, might was the way to live, and soon evil leaders gathered mindless but strong followers. Power came to the most numerous and best equipped armies that spread famine, disease, death, and war all around the known globe.

Through the ages various styles of governments were established and called the shots for many different civilizations. Women and children have had little value to ruthless dictators and their armies. Consequently, the devil was bringing millions of weak, uneducated, sinful individuals into hell with him.

But "when the time had fully come, God sent his son, born of a woman (the family component) and born under law" (Galatians 4:4) to redeem a people of His own! HE would shed HIS perfect blood to cleanse their sin! Then later God sent the Spirit of his Son into the hearts of those who would believe and accept the Creator's great love for them (John 3:16). HE would show HIS purpose in sparing life by placing believing people into HIS own Family. HE would set free anyone who would soften their heart as they remembered the sacrifices of God's "only begotten Son". This was a demonstration of real parental love for HIS own – those who would believe and trust a Heavenly Father.

In this second Unit, I want to dig deeper into the power of our sin nature and the effect of shame on dysfunctional children. Plus, I wish to share how Satan has weakened the influence of parents in America through the generations. Then we will look at the impact that "Flawed Parents" have on their children's self-image. In the last chapter I inserted a powerful story of how God's grace was able to rebuild a Chaotic family.

Chapter 4

SECRETS OF THE SOUL ANALYZED

No doubt you are already aware that every human being is made of three parts.

THE BODY

The body can be seen and felt. It consists of an outward envelope (skin and hair) and multiple inner parts that function to keep us alive and moving. We try to protect, improve, and keep our bodies healthy. Our response to cravings and temptations is most often demonstrated through our physical bodies.

THE SOUL

The soul (*psyche*) is primarily the mind and is seen in three areas of interest.

1) The *intellect* where we learn, discern, and compile data to make choices and determine directions. These choices often respond to the needs and demands of the body.

2) Then there are our *emotions* which often determine how the intellect is used. The mind reacts to situations around us, our feelings, or the habits and convictions we've learned. The soul can be downcast (Psalm 42:11) or joyful (Psalm 94:19), and it is seen through the actions of our body, which can honor God or dishonor him. When we displease our Lord, we usually humiliate ourselves and degrade our own witness.

3) Lastly there is the *volition* in the soul, which melds together our feelings, emotions, and all that we have learned. Here we establish a course that we determine to be the best direction for our lives. And in this, we Christians commit our minds to Love and serve the Lord with all our soul (Joshua 22:5).

The soul is the real part of our "inmost being" (Psalm 103:1) and it lives forever (Matthew 25:46, John 5:28-29). Jesus says it is possible for someone to forfeit his soul by being wrapped up in material things. Matthew 16:26 reminds the believer to resist worldly temptations, as we discussed in chapter 3 lest we forfeit the potential for which the soul was created. Jesus also promises that rewards will be given at the end of life in keeping with how people used their bodies and minds. The saved soul will receive a new glorified body (Philippians 3:21). However, the condemned soul will suffer in great heat with some form of spiritual body for eternity! (Mark 9:43c, 48).

I am convinced that the many references in the Bible to the heart are actually talking about the soul. A good definition for the heart is: the inner man, seat of all passions, desires, affections, and endeavors. The heart is also the essence of personality, and the functioning mind.[5] Peter calls the humble attraction of a person's character, "the hidden person of the heart" (I Peter 3:4 NKJV). And it's the place in us that God searches and tests (I Samuel 16:7b, Jeremiah 17:10). This word (*cardia* In the Greek) has to be a synonym for soul!

THE SPIRIT

"For who among men knows the thoughts of a man except the man's spirit within him?" (I Corinthians 2:11) I understand our little "s" spirit to be the God consciousness that every person is born with. This is the part of the brain that longs to be helped or guided by a spiritual being who is most often invisible. Here is where many lost souls are led astray by Satan's counterfeit religions, New Age thinking, or even demonic worship (including seances, levitation, or deep trances). This is how a person can say he is "spiritual" but not be a Christian.

In a more positive light, the spirit is the part of us that is regenerated when we accept Jesus Christ as our personal Savior. The King James Bible calls it "quickened" or made alive (Ephesians 2:1, 5). This is how we are "born again" in John 3 when the Holy Spirit comes to live inside us. (See also Romans 8:9, how we know we belong to Christ).

It is my conviction that the references in Scripture to the conscience refer to this spirit, which is the third part of the human trilogy. For the conscience is the place in the frontal lobe of the brain where we sense

---

[5] *Zondervan Encyclopedia of the Bible*, Volume 3, Zondervan Publishing House, Grand Rapids, MI, 1975, 58

and begin to develop awareness of right or wrong. In Romans 8:16, we read: "The Holy Spirit testifies (explains) with our spirit we are children of God." Our new living spirit has the power with God to "put to death the misdeeds of the body" which are caused by the sin nature (8:13). So, in our born-again spirit or cleansed conscience we have the guidance and strength to resist temptation, overcome guilty feelings, and rise above our difficult family situations.

This supernatural power inside our brains can work with our soul to determine emotionally or rationally the godly way to deal with dysfunctional issues. Although Paul in Romans 7 says we go back and forth in our decisions to please the Lord or please our old self, the quickened spirit can control us if we yield to it. A daily fully yielded spirit can experience a "resurrected" life, like Jesus (Romans 6:5). The secret is asking God to constantly make us aware of how to follow the truths in 6:12-14.

Do not let sin reign in your mortal body so that you obey its evil desires. Do not offer the parts of your body to sin, as instruments of wickedness, but rather offer yourselves to God, as those who have been brought from death to life. And offer the parts of your body to him as instruments of righteousness. For sin shall not be your master.

Again, I'm talking about the potential God-thinking that is placed in our minds at birth. Plus, we should see the way man's soul and spirit are so connected yet individual in their role. For our spiritual enemy finds ways to cause us to take deliberate acts of selfishness, greed, and rebellion. This regularly brings about a searing or corrupting of the conscience (I Timothy 4:2; Titus 1:15) if we offer our minds or bodies to those "evil desires".

Perhaps you are uncomfortable with my trichotomy explanation here. That's OK. Many theologians believe the soul and spirit are not only fully connected but are a single entity. Nevertheless, you'll agree with me that our soul is involved with our daily decisions to do right or to do wrong. Within the soul and mind, we have both a sinful nature and a new nature that need to be controlled by the Spirit of Christ (Romans 8:9). We believe that before a person comes to know Jesus personally, he or she is totally controlled by that sinful nature. Each of us at one time were there, "darkened in our understanding and separated from the life of God because of ignorance due to the hardening of [our] hearts" (Ephesians 4:18). Your spiritual heart or soul was at one time separated from God and hardened to his ways. The intellect, emotions, and will of the soul are poisoned at birth, a consequence of Adam and Eve's fall (Romans 5:12).

All parents of dysfunction have that sin nature. Many are controlled by it constantly, blinded by the devil's work (2 Corinthians 4:4). But then, many born-again people move in and out of its power (a carnal Christian -1 Corinthians 3:3). But the sin nature is the cause of all the cruelty, danger, misunderstanding, and neglect that precious children face in their homes. When a back-slidden believer follows the ways of the world (1 John 2:15-16) instead of the Holy Spirit; he or she can become very self-centered and greedy - pursuing one of the temptations of the Flawed Parents just described in Chapters 2 and 3.

Romans 8:7-8 describes the unsaved as having a rebellious soul that cannot submit to God or please him. Many non-Christian parents do not feel promptings in their conscience to sympathize with their children's fearful feelings nor to understand the importance of inquiring regularly about what their children are thinking or wanting.

However, I have found that if a kind parent had a good moral upbringing or was influenced by gracious and caring people along the way, their personality could possibly lead them to be patient and gentle with their kids even though the Holy Spirit is not dwelling within them. The natural limited love of man as made in God's image (Genesis 1:27) can cause some unsaved people to earnestly provide, protect, and even honestly cuddle their infants and toddlers. This soft soul may be open at times to God's draw. *We pastors should be looking for this as we talk to the grandparents, the parents, the teens, or even the younger children.* It is amazing how little unsaved people know about Jesus' great love for them. And it's so unfortunate that many adults have never come to realize how HE actually descended from Heaven to make them ready to spend eternity with God the Father! They could be made whole people now, able to use all three parts of themselves to demonstrate the image of God comfortably and correctly.

But then there are the cold, antagonistic folks who are working against the potential good of the family. These lost people are all about themselves. Their minds are far away from God, and they are not desiring to change. *If only we or someone else could lead them to the Savior. We need to be open to that possibility and make the presenting of the gospel as clear as possible in our counseling times.*

He that wins souls is wise (Proverbs 11:30, NKJV). As Paul says, with the indwelling Holy Spirit in control, the true believer can count himself dead to sin (Romans 6:11). So, it is *our responsibility, dear reader, to show our counselees who are suffering with dysfunction that we have a tried and proven answer from the Bible for their serious dilemma, and that we believe it wholeheartedly.* The Lord Jesus Christ wants very much to give each of them "rest for their souls" (Matthew 11:29). We know that if "the Spirit of God lives in (them)" (Romans 8:9a), damaged people can be changed and controlled by HIM instead of by evil spirits. They will have the power to get victory over anger, bitterness, depression, confusion, and rebellion. *As counselors, we can help them find or rediscover their Savior and then their peace.*

Any temptation or habitual sin can be overcome when a person submits to the all mighty and all loving God to guide and speak through them. And this could begin with any individual in the three generations of the broken family. Hard hearts and selfish moods can certainly be changed when the Spirit of truth and love is in control. For as you also well know, "The Word of God is alive and active. It penetrates soul and spirit...and judges the thoughts and attitudes of the heart" (Hebrews 4:12). *The Word of God that we share with the right person at the right time can soften the troubled heart and tenderize a wrong mood of either the trouble- maker or the victim of dysfunction.* God alone can suddenly or gradually change the tough thoughts and revolting feelings people are subjected to.

THE SIN NATURE OF THE FLAWED

I ask myself why the **Controlling** Parent is so critical and vicious. I see not only the temptation of loving himself too much, but also the sin of wanting to exercise most of the power in the house. But I also believe that his sin nature says in his mind (soul) "I am the most important person here. Without me and my money this family would not survive. So, I have the right to be served." In pride, deep down inside, he/she enjoys the authority and expects to keep it. This futile thinking is forming a hard heart. (Ephesians 4:17)

When studying the **Conforming** Adult, it appears that she must persuade her children to do what she really thinks is best for them. Perhaps without realizing it she pushes herself to possess them (remember chapter 3). Although the temptation of materialism is her means of operation; her real pride problem is she wants to be noticed by others, and to have people outside the home admire her life work! This also is futile thinking supplied by the "old nature" that brings about a loss of sensitivity (Ephesians 4:18).

Now the sin nature for **Coddlers** is the unwillingness to exercise any control. Their faulty reasoning is "If I give them everything they want, they will be happier, feel safer, and will love and respect me more." But the purpose of the parent is not to be a best friend, but to be a best example. "Train a child in the way he should go, and when he is old, he will not turn from it" (Proverbs 22:6, KJV). Children need order. Mom and dad then will correctly teach them about what they need, not what they want. But this weak parent wants to be liked because his self-esteem is low. This adult will not strive for what's best, for in her secret mind she's not worthy to have it or show it.

The fourth flawed parent, the **Chaotic**, as you may recall, has little self-discipline and is always looking for the easy route. This person's sin against God is not caring to discover what his or her own real purpose in life is. He will teach his children to go with the flow and look for free stuff. Life will control her rather than the other way around. Since the parents were never built up or valued as a child, they can find

> " *The purpose of the parent is not to be a best friend, but a best example.* "

nothing to strive for themselves. Neither can they supply anything to encourage their own kids to achieve in life. Without a reason to excel or even do their best, there will be little to inspire their children to greater heights. These adults have never learned or have forgotten that God sincerely loves them just as He made them. As His creation they are worth enough for Jesus to come and die for them. To live as lost is to gratify the cravings of our sinful nature and follow its desires and thoughts. "But because of His great love for us, God, who is rich in mercy, made us alive with Christ even when we were dead in transgressions" (Ephesians 2:3-4). *As counselors we need to get around to sharing this verse with the chaotic parent and/or their children when we are working with them. Expressing passion and sincerity, we can apply the truths to their situation.* Jesus will give them value and sure reason to reach for more.[6]

In discussing the power of the "old man" and how each dysfunctional parent was affected in a different way to sin against their families, I asked a Christian College Psychology Professor if he saw a common denominator here. What is it that causes each of these flawed parents to develop these negative and demeaning traits? Are they trying to compensate for something they also were damaged by in their childhood? Dr. Edgington answered with what I was trying to conclude in my mind. "It's their self-esteem! Each one in their own way is striving to have what they missed before they became parents. They all want to be acknowledged or liked or considered important by others around them! These 'flawed parents' as you call them, are pressing to deal with a poor self-image. Deep inside they are trying to cover for embarrassment or shame of their past."[7]

---

[6] Robert S. McGee, *The Search for Significance*, Rapha Publishing, Houston, TX, 1990, 41.

[7] Interview with Dr. Thomas Edgington, Grace College, Winona Lake, IN August 2023.

Breaking this down further, **Controllers** will not let anyone get close enough to see who they are inside. The **Conformer** is making up rules to look wise and strong, because they didn't feel value before. The **Coddler** wishes she had been given more freedom in the past but feels undeserving of it. And the **Chaotic** person bought into the lies that they were unworthy of any respect or praise. So, they misrun their lives and their families seeking more appreciation or approval, although not expecting it. They likewise need a stronger self-worth.

However ironically, each of these flawed parents does not understand that they are stealing life's most needed respect and value away from the ones they should care about. But because of their own seriously wounded self-image, they cannot see that they are forcefully or uncaringly pushing away the offspring and/or mate that naturally wants to love them.

As a reminder, we are all born with a sin nature! As you read in chapter 3, like Adam and Eve, we all fall for Satan's temptations. He knows which area we are weakest in. *Sin is our desire to run our life our way.* "You will not surely die, the serpent said to the woman. For God knows when you eat from it your eyes will be opened and you will be like God, knowing good and evil" (Genesis 3:4-5). That really means having within us the power or privilege to decide what is wrong. And that power is of opinions formed from our own sin-tainted eyes. We even go so far as to desire or strive to make foolish choices and to live on the edge with pride and wickedness.

Then also because of weakness and yielding to their sin nature, people allow others to suppress the truth for them. Atheists and agnostics will lie about God's revelation and ignore His power. So, with occasional doubt, many will not honor and thank Him (Romans 1:18b, 21).

Thus, folks who are not open to spiritual things repeatedly make the decision, whether purposefully or subconsciously, to turn away from the light that would make a big difference (see John 3:19-20). That is the tremendous negative impact that sin has on the human intellect, emotions, and will.

DECISION: TO GROW OR NOT

Now let us return to the lead character of this book. Jeff learned subconsciously from his father to be a **Controlling** Parent. But when he became a Christian, he had the potential within his soul-spirit—the indwelling Holy Spirit—to forsake that wrongful and selfish way of looking at his God-given children. As a dad he didn't change as much as he could have because the battle between the "new man" and the "old man" was very real. The Apostle Paul says that believers must be obedient to their new Master and be willing to allow HIM to help them. "In regard to your former way of life, put off your old self, which is being corrupted by its deceitful desires" (Ephesians 4:22).

Jeff was not ready to yield that much of his life to God. He still had some scores to settle. Primarily, he wanted to prove to his dad and other relatives that he could be more successful than his own alcoholic father. His "corrupted" mind from childhood was dealing with the stronghold of pride. He had sincerely repented of his past mistakes and evil acts, yet with a bit of self-importance he thought he could now make a better life for himself in his own strength. With God on his side, he could proceed with a more productive life and be respected as a clean, self-controlled, and honest man in this new positive Christian atmosphere. Unfortunately, this dream never happened, He could not overcome the wrong image of himself, because of the secret shame and guilt he felt from his struggle with bitterness and hatred for his cruel dad.

Instead, Satan's temptations of worldly possessions and do-it-your-self power gained much influence in his immature spirit and soul. The Holy Spirit's pull to humble Jeff more and to trust his new Heavenly Father is what he really needed to learn about and submit to.

Although we were trying to teach him that God's way of growth was much better than the world's way of achievement, Jeff was not willing to let go of what his bitter, usually intoxicated father had engrained in his mind. "If you're going to make anything of yourself, son, work hard, watch your back, and get yours before they get you."

Jeff could not trust people, not his new Christian brothers and not even his new loving Heavenly Father. He was not ready to understand love. He never had it, never felt it, never knew how to experience it. Members of a dysfunctional family are unable to genuinely care for others before doing for themselves. At the time I did not realize how deep his chaotic upbringing had twisted his reasoning. Even though we had some talks about his feelings and what was most important in life; Jeff was not capable of fully opening up to me. Had I really understood what was missing in his heart (soul), how he was being controlled by those wicked "deceitful desires" (of covering his shame) without his even knowing it; then I would have taught him differently. Even after watching him try to beat his wife and swindle me for an automobile in the late 70s, I didn't realize how the devil was working through the pattern of a dysfunctional lifestyle. Our real enemy was trying to cause me to give up on this new raw Christian. And I almost did, twice!

The usual discipleship training of learning who Jesus is, what the Holy Spirit can do for us, how to pray and read our Bibles, and why it's

71

important to find a Bible-believing church and good Christian friends, is not enough for new believers battling serious wrongs of the past. I know now that there was another more significant path of training that this man who grew up under a "Controlling Father" needed to pursue slowly and persistently. His hidden feeling of shame and worthlessness needed to be talked about so he could discover how valuable he was to God and to other saved people.

Therefore, let us consider that the weight of past hurt and haunting memories of fear keeps many new Christians from growing in Christ and becoming "like God in true righteousness" (Ephesians 4:24). Like me at that time, most church leaders still don't fully understand the terrible impact of a past tumultuous home-life on young Christian adults who are now trying to start their own families with better standards and principles. Perhaps these wounded newer believers have accepted Christ in college or found their faith while feeling alone and dealing with new trials. Maybe, because they are now raising their own children, they feel the need to get serious with their invisible but revealing Heavenly Father.

We must seek the Holy Spirit's guidance to help these precious unwitting believers to deal with some hard to understand and never-talked-about issues of the past. In writing this chapter, I want us to consider that many 30–45-year-old adults are still ashamed of their parents. After

" The weight of past ...haunting memories keeps Christians from growing in Christ. "

all this time they continue to incorrectly feel guilty that they themselves may have been the cause of or major contributors to the addictions, divorce, or relational trauma that took place for years in their houses. Born anew now, and with a softer, more loving heart, perhaps they feel their previous rebellion or angry words of retaliation just made things worse since there was no real resolution.

A RELATIONSHIP WITH GOD MAKES A PERSON NEW

The putting on of the "new self" is a continual and difficult process of spiritual growth that takes time and deliberate steps to "renew the mind" and to "be transformed" from the ways of the world (see Romans 12:2). Coming from a terrible home life, Jeff, shortly after his conversion, needed to understand some significant biblical truths about God's work and how HE helps us change. Regeneration means a totally new life. Second Corinthians 5:17 says "Old things have passed away; behold, all things have become new" (NKJV). But the flesh holds on strong, and many new believers will not shake it and allow the Holy Spirit to control their thinking and emotions. My disciple back then would only give in so much. He needed more sympathetic reasoning with definite timely, on-the-spot answers in the transforming process; not just hard fast goals to push for. That is also a part of hands-on discipleship.

Since he did not understand or trust real love, Jeff was unable to demonstrate it and to pass it on to his wife or his children. This man was not sure God could actually love him personally. As with many new converts with past family problems, he had to learn that his Heavenly Father was so different from his earthly father.

Millions of Christian men cannot accept the teaching of God as Heavenly Father, because of the verbal or physical abuse of their paternal parents or stepdads. Likewise, our congregations have young women who have difficulty relating to their husbands emotionally and intimately because they were sexually abused by a father, a mother's boyfriend, or their own older brother. *We spiritual leaders should read about, study, and prayerfully ponder how to teach, correct, and train in righteousness (see 2 Timothy 3:16) to help our friends heal from those traumatic memories through the powerful Word of the Lord and HIS Holy Spirit.*

Many professional Christian Counselors explain that the resistance a person has - to recognizing God as their "Heavenly Father" - is a barrier they have erected in their aching mind. "The reason for the barrier needs to be addressed, the hurt talked about" with a mature, caring listener. Wounded believers can face their difficult feelings by asking the Lord to walk with them as they try to pardon or at least work through the pain that a cruel or an emotionally sick dad caused (more specifics in Chapter 8). "God is able to replace these bitter or fearful emotions with HIS love."[8] Remembering that Jesus lovingly, purposefully, and willingly died for them at Calvary can supply the inner strength to keep going with a healed heart. "Allowing God then to be their real Father makes it possible for HIM to be the real Healer." The victim can then enter the Lord's rest and be comforted and accept that HE is always trustworthy.[9] God promised to never leave HIS Child no matter what doubt they may still have or how strong their remaining anger might be.

---

[8] Janet M. Lerner, *Restoring Families*, Facilitator's Guide Living Free, Chattanooga, TN, 2000, 10-11
[9] Ibid, 3

Because of such serious fatherly abuse, countless American children grow up thinking that their life is not worth much. They have been dealing with a sense of failure or rejection or shame for a long time in their families from parental criticism, insensitivity, even physical harm. As a result, when they are teens or young adults, they have a very poor self-image, and they not only feel inferior to others in the family, but they feel hopeless of ever improving. Most of us know that merciful love from GOD and the sacrifice of HIS only SON for our individual souls is what makes a person feel valuable and created with purpose.

We then are called to help children of dysfunction to realize there is a biblical way to deal with shame over bad memories from the past. Guilt and regret are God-created mental impressions in the conscience (little 's' spirit) that notify people of things that are not complete nor settled over an experience or encounter from the past. This comes especially if they feel or are told that the problem was mainly their own doing. Then, as the wounded person thinks more about, even dwells on that negative experience, a painful realization will settle in their mind. The emotion of shame is felt when he cannot overcome the embarrassment or remorse of his regrettable actions. This shame can produce a paralyzing fear that causes negative characteristics like inferiority, self-pity, passiveness, or isolation to take over in the mind and rule the choices of the victim (Christian or not).

We can show those confused and hurting with shame that diligent study of God's word, and interacting with other believers can help them understand how God values His children. This will take away most feelings of shame and greatly improve the believer's self-worth.[10]

---

[10] Robert S. McGee, *Search for Significance*, Rapha Publishing, Houston, TX, 1990, 103.

Because God with unfailing love has forgiven all who have repented of their sin, there is no reason to feel condemned (Romans 8:1). Born again Christians must allow God's Holy Spirit within to show them just who they are in HIS eyes. They have a new identity after accepting Jesus as their Savior. The saved sufferers should now believe they are greatly and eternally valued by HIM. Their own self-worth must be based on God's realistic opinion of them! Because of Christ's redemption and resurrection, they have become worthy, forgiven, loved, accepted, and complete in HIM.[11]

This truthful way of pondering just who we are - is how we defeat the feelings of shame and guilt. As all believers should refuse to accept Satan's lies about condemnation from our failings and unworthiness; they can demolish that false pretension that keeps them down mentally and spiritually (more in chapter 9)! *Thus, people we encounter need to understand they are significant and precious to God. That also makes them important and special to us leaders.*

So, individuals from dysfunctional families nearly always have a struggle with self-esteem, except perhaps for those born with the hero personality. Yet most of the survivors in those homes will never feel good enough for others outside to appreciate or love them. They might become proficient at covering up their fears or anxieties, but they will always be pressing and pushing to look good or to find some kind of success in their lives. We have not been created to prove ourselves worthy. Life is not about making good impressions or being someone that we are not.

In 1 John 4:16-18 we are assured that walking in Christ's love can persuade us that neither the fear of rejection nor judgment for our sin is the real problem. But our guilt or worry does often hold us back. I

---

[11] Ibid, 108.

"We have not been created to prove ourselves worthy."

repeat, these negative feelings can be conquered through understanding our Lord's overwhelming and complete redemption for us on the Cross. By claiming the Bible's clear explanation of God's love for us and why HE took our punishment; we have confidence that HE is listening to us and will answer our prayers (Hebrews 4:16). Therefore, worry or frustration can no longer build up more fear in our minds. HIS "perfect love casts out fear" (1 John 4:18). By meditating on the promise of this verse, we shall be set free.

COMBINING OUR PROVEN FACTS

So now, we must see that we can effectively combine the methods and experiences of Christian experts in psychology with the directives of Scripture. Counselors well versed in theology can share that God placed valuable principles for the human brain and feelings of the soul in His Word. We are to glean these nuggets of truth from the Bible and apply them to the issues and problems that cause behavioral traps.

I know that God heals and wants us to bring our worst emotional and relational pain to HIM for peace and hope. Psalm 23:4-6 gives needed advice for when we are going through a mental valley that shadows our end, a condition that seems like there is no way out! We are to recognize our Lord's presence and decide not to be afraid! HE promises to comfort us with a "rod and staff". The rod is an instrument of authority. For the Christian it is the Bible filled with valuable principles to help us. And the staff is the Counselor who shows the troubled person how and where to apply those nuggets of truth to his/her very confusing situation.

God wants to "prepare" a victorious banquet for the sufferer of a dysfunctional family after the successful battle against an enemy. *So, with sound biblical counseling and the right words of guidance, better thinking can begin to bring serious change to the soul.* Sometimes helping our mistreated folks connect with mental health providers who are evangelical Christians is an important additional step.

There is one more thought to make clear. My many references to poor self-esteem in this chapter are not to say a person should learn to love him or herself more. I'm not talking about self-love but self-respect. When the Bible says we are to love others as much as we love ourselves, it is not saying we should lift up our looks or achievements in prideful admiration. We should not be thinking in narcissistic ways or worshiping ourselves more than anyone or anything else. Paul is teaching that we are to respect the person God has made for Himself. Since we are greatly loved and very important to our Creator (as has been clearly explained thus far), we must do what we can to protect our well-designed bodies, souls, and spirits. It is important to appreciate ourselves as the Lord's amazing intention. We can be astounded at what God did in individually creating us, at the wonderful talents HE has given us, and at the opportunities to minister to others that He has provided us. Yet we must constantly remember that life is about uplifting our Merciful Lord, not the self-centered Me. "It is not self-love that a mature believer needs, but self-respect!"[12]

---

[12] Dennis Prager, Prager U. Fireside Chat Podcast #248, July 2022.

As we talk about sin and the impact it has on parents' decisions, it should be acknowledged that we all need help in dealing with our past. Then, our weak but reasonable ability to choose what is best for our future needs to be based on a Biblical worldview. Our God wants to give us the power to make right choices that will benefit our families. If we trust him and believe what he says, we will receive wisdom from His Word to deal with mistakes, overcome serious temptations, and demolish strongholds that capture our minds. Take some time now in the following chart to observe how self-image affects the four flawed parents and the way they raise their children.

CHART FOR FLAWED PARENTS

NAME	TRAITS	PATTERN	FLAW	TREATED KIDS	SIN	NEEDED to BE
CONTROLLING	Loud, bossy	Dominate	Forcing, Compliance	Criticize, push	Me first, Selfish	Appreciated as a person
CONFORMING	Too orderly, Operate smooth	Lead well	Possessive, Perfection	Manipulate, Pressure	Me best, Conceited	Admired for acts
CODDLING	Over giving, Buys gifts	Make happy	Spoil, Be friends with	Money, Ease	Children first, avoid complaints	Provided for, Safe
CHAOTIC	No plan, Carefree	To each his own	No discipline, Guideless	Little care, On their own	Me #1, Lazy	Loved as individual

This chart is designed to help the Reader put together the characteristics of each of the 4 "Flawed Parents". You will notice as you look across the rows, each column or description builds on the previous one. For instance, as I pointed out in the first 4 chapters, the Controlling Dad is loud and bossy, wants to dominate every situation, and will force the kids to comply through criticism. The reason he is so self-centered is in the last column. He was never appreciated by his parents when he was at home. So, in his bitterness he decided at a young age that he would work his way to the top, and never allow anyone to push him around! To be appreciated in his mind meant forcing people to respect him for what he did – at work or at home! His "flaw" came about from what he missed growing up!

The same can be said about the other three weak dads and moms, as you follow the rows horizontally from left to right.

A future chart after chapter 7 on "Agape Love" will illustrate what their negative trait will do to the family, how the counselor can help the parent to see his/her issue, and then to look at a potential positive result that all can work towards.

Chapter 5

THE DEVIL'S ATTACK ON OUR NATION

Let's review what we've discussed in the first unit and fourth chapter where we:

- Explained and defined the Dysfunctional Family.
- Exposed its afflicters, showing the four main "Flawed Parents."
- Looked carefully at its victims from the view of the four roles that kids play in these situations.
- Dealt with the devil's role in lying temptations to steal away the goodness and love that God intended for the family.
- And in the last chapter, we covered how and why shame, guilt, and poor self-image builds in a dysfunctional family.

Now, this chapter goes further to reveal Satan's work in destroying the strong, familiar family in our America. This Liar and enemy of

God's people continues to attack long established moral values, biblical principles, government rules, higher education, and peoples' freedoms.

Before the sexual revolution of the 1960s, the productive adults of the United States had moral moorings, sought to keep the law, found honesty and integrity of great importance, and desired to be the best examples for their beloved children, as well as their best teachers. They also wanted to do the same for their neighbors' children. Trying to be good parents was natural. Following the Golden Rule and the good principles that Jesus taught were worth striving for as an adult pattern.

But our American society in the 2020s is far different. There appear to be more mothers and fathers who do not want to be or know how to be good parents now. One poll I read states that Americans feel that about 70% of our families are dysfunctional.[13]

In the early 1980s Doctor James Dobson was the first to speak out about this deteriorating problem. He organized a ministry called *Focus on the Family* and spread the word all over America via radio broadcasts, books, and speaking engagements. His emphasis was "The family is under attack." He addressed the problems of loose morals, lack of discipline, an exceedingly greedy culture, humanistic philosophy in higher education, and even of a great deficiency of practical teaching on parenthood. Over the years his work has had a great impact and has helped to preserve many families.

As a pastor and marriage counselor, I have discovered over time that there has clearly been a well-organized and specifically designed plan to destroy the family in America and to alter our society so that it is out of control. The hidden goal has been to change our country into a secular,

---

[13] Forbes Magazine, Saul Gourani, November 2019.

atheistic, amoral, anarchist, and personal rights-oriented world - all definitions of a socialistic form of government. All these things combined plus crime, poverty, the street drug-opioid battle, aggressive politics, and outright demonism have broken our families apart and pushed them past the time of correction. In many cases there is no hope. Each generation since the 60s has grown worse.

Grade schoolteachers are finding more and more selfish, unruly, and irresponsible children who refuse to be taught and have little or no respect for adults in authority. This is true now in rural communities as well as the urban settings of America. Many national surveys and public interviews are showing unhealthy and disappointing results that prove our families are falling apart quicker than we want to admit. Let me share some alarming statistics about the loss of loving parental care that have been compiled over more than 50 years from 1960 to 2015 in America:

- Children living with two parents in their first marriage consisted of 73% of households in 1960. By 1990 it had dropped to 55%, and in the census of 2010 only 40% of our children lived with their original parents.
- The portion of children born outside of marriage in America in 1960 was only 5%, but by 2015 it had jumped to 42% (nearly half of the babies born that year).
- One parent raising kids in 1960 was just 9% of families. But the figure in 1990 was 21%, and by 2015 single parenting had gone up to 40% of all households. [14]

---

[14] Chris Segrin & Jeanne Flora, *Family Communication*, Routledge Publications 2004.

DISRUPT THEN DESTROY

To me this shows that a concerted effort has been made to disrupt and ruin the American family. Some experts blame poverty, others "no-fault" divorce, and still others attribute the problem to rampant drug use and city gangs. I see still another cause—politics. For instance, the recent public disclosure of The Black Lives Matter Manifesto states as one of their goals: "to rid the country of the archaic nuclear family and promote families of all sorts in support of the gay-rights agenda."[15]

But even before that group became popular, liberal lawyers and atheistic politicians were working to destroy the teaching of Christian principles. Teachers' unions continue to push for total control of school children through the full power of local principals and school board leaders. These humanist-minded educators have lessened disciplinary action in school, took prayer and the Pledge of Allegiance out, and even promoted vulgar and sexually explicit books and videos in the libraries - of elementary schools!

Currently, left-leaning politicians and liberally educated teachers are strongly promoting critical race theory and even favor allowing teenage females to get abortions without telling their parents. They continue to confuse young minds with the theory that there is no absolute truth in our world any longer. Liberal teachers in education and ACLU lawyers say that to think the same moral values are applicable for every person and every environment and culture today is old-fashioned, foolish, and unscientific

---

[15] Glenbeck.com, *Discovering Black Lives Plot to Destroy the Family* Glenn TV, July 16, 2020.

"*They confuse young minds with the theory that there is no absolute truth.*"

From this view has come alternate teachings in many universities that:

- A conservative government should have no power to prohibit abortion. It's a woman's right to choose.
- Judeo-Christian views on life should not be allowed to be presented on college campuses; they should be treated as "misinformation."
- The Caucasian race is predisposed to prejudice. Racism is a systemic problem. And children need to be introduced to this real point in the public schools.
- The US Constitution needs to be fluent and rewritten to fit with today's trends.
- Principles from the Bible must be confined to religious institutions. Those organizations must be limited in their proselytizing in our secular society and policed, labeling their teaching as possible hate speech.
- Alternate forms of government should be presented in schools. A democratic form of socialism should be explained and promoted as a needed change here in America.

And from this rather strong liberal philosophy in higher education has come the mysterious work of the increase in the power of the

Federal Government. This could very likely result in the loss of some of the rights of free citizens, and possibly bring great persecution for Christians.

This reminds me of the powerful one-world government, antichrist, and false prophet all prophesied in the Revelation 13. As an Evangelical Bible-believing Christian, I feel strongly that our Lord Jesus is coming back soon. As many preachers predict, the end times are upon us. All the signs of Matthew 24 are happening. We are now living in the historical period when Israel became a nation again (1948) and obtained political power over Jerusalem (1967). Nothing more needs to take place before the Rapture happens! All this is another reason why we must look for people we can help among our flocks that are living as "Dysfunctional Families" in these end times.

A LOOK AT GENERATIONAL DETERIORATION

Let me share some additional ideas about how the family in the USA has become worse over the last five generations. My Dad was of the Builders Generation. Born in 1929, his peers were not only very patriotic and had good manners, but they were also strongly family oriented. In fact, anyone who was part of a divorced or publicly discredited family was looked down upon by society and felt sorry for by Christians.

People my age, the Baby Boomers, rebelled against the establishment, wanted their freedom to do as they pleased with their bodies (as teenagers), and questioned all authority. Suddenly, a philosophy of rebellion and doing things differently, penetrated the views of everyone in American society. Resistance to the Vietnam War, assassinations of government leaders, expansion of marijuana use, and violent race relations all brought about great anger and fear in our nation. Soon a spirit of "throw out the old fashioned" filled the minds of everyone 30 and under.

In time the Boomer generation would raise their own children without rules. In the late 70s spanking was ridiculed. So, most of our kids were spoiled and were not held accountable for their behavior. In addition, they were taught to question the words of teachers and preachers.

When the Baby Busters, born between 1965 and 1980, were little they became latch-key kids because women were now going to work in droves. So, there were several hours of time between school closing and parents getting home for supper. Thus, many houses of Busters were forced to raise themselves. As a result, video games, youthful smoking, and staying up late and partying became the norm for the teens.

When this Generation X became parents though, they wanted to right the many societal and environmental wrongs; yet they still pushed themselves greedily to make lots of money. Although many good preschool nurseries were created to care for and educate the children of working mothers, relationships between parents and their children sometimes became poor and sparse. There just was not enough time allowed nor willingness demonstrated by the many Flawed Parents to nurture or train the next generation well.

Likewise, it seems that being married was less and less important, and marriages were becoming more and more difficult to maintain. Live-in couples filled our city apartments and college dorms, so their homes looked very different. When they were present, parents were poor role-models, and many selfish ones did not care.

The Millennials (Gen Y, 1981- 2000) then turned to the Internet and social media for opinions on the family and what was right and wrong. They were bombarded in public school with sex education and homosexual rights. By now, families were defined as just about anything, not just single parents, but neighbors raising others' kids, many different boyfriends babysitting mom's children from different dads. Even married male couples began adopting and raising girls. Morals and religious principles were ignored or forgotten.

As parents then, Gen Y adults made up their own rules and tried to live out what they had learned in universities. They were taught that there is no definite good or bad, and fair or unfair is only relevant according to the circumstances in which you find yourself.

OTHER PROOFS OF SPIRITUAL ATTACK ON FAMILIES

As a result, society has changed significantly. Tradition and authority are constantly being challenged by each younger generation. For instance, we now see that socialism has been taught to the age group in high school and college. So, a high percentage of people in their late 20s and 30s (Millennials) are now interested in having their college loans paid off by the government. They are making white people in America feel guilty for the race problems we have had for three centuries. They favor giving illegals free health care and the right to vote. This generation progressively promotes transgender philosophies. They want to limit the number of people who are incarcerated for even serious crimes. But none of these liberal views encouraged through their education will help the families they are pretending to raise.

It is no wonder that among the many mixed up groups of people inhabiting the same house today, the Centennials (Gen Z), (those born from 2000 up to this writing) are confused about what is best or who is right. Many young adults have no plans to get married and have watched their older brothers and sisters return home broken-hearted because of fractured relationships.

Medical experts tell us there are far more children with mental illnesses today than in the 90s and early 2000s. This includes bi-polar and schizophrenia issues, depression and anxiety, and now even "gender paralysis". Public schools in most urban centers are war zones. They are producing very low-test scores; and good, serious teachers, investing in the children's success, are scarce.

What I want to make clear is that our America has become more hateful, immoral, selfish, rights-centered, and politically crooked than in earlier generations. Too many weak parents have been caught up in racism, protests, lawsuits, political causes, and cultural wars, whether liberal or conservative. All this is at the expense of neglecting the needs and interests of their own children. It is no wonder that dysfunction abounds now in every community.

Satan tried to destroy the family at the very beginning. He talked Eve into acting in disobedience to God. As result of their fall, Adam failed to lead Eve or their boys, and Lucifer took advantage of the aggressive personality of Cain and filled him with jealousy and pride. The Apostle John explained it well in his first letter: "And why did he (Cain) murder him? Because his own actions were evil, and his brothers were righteous" (1 John 3:12). That describes jealousy and pride very well.

Satan's role is pointed out in verse 8 of the same chapter "The one who does what is sinful is of the devil, because the devil has been sinning from the beginning." Then Cain showed anger, and anger leads to hatred, and hatred breeds murder (v.15). God warned Cain, but Satan's work prevailed in the second man's heart. "Sin is crouching at your door" (Genesis 4:7). Sin ruled Cain instead of Cain ruling his emotions and ferocious action. This is the devil's plan of attack for all of us. He plays with our emotions to capture us and control us to do his bidding. Remember my explanation of the soul in chapter 3? Intellectually, Cain thought the clean vegetables were better than bloody animals. Emotionally, he was angry with whom he thought was a mysterious and demanding God. Volitionally, his jealousy of his brother caused Cain to hate Abel and to get rid of him. Yet, God's earlier word to him could have set him free from his sinful action.

The Apostle John gives us hope and a definitive answer to uncontrolled emotion. Giving more of our decision-making to Christ is how we get the strength to resist the temptations of the devil. The reason the Son of God appeared was to destroy the devil's work (3:8b) The Son of God is always the answer to the power of fear and the enemy's attacks. "For God does not give us the spirit of timidity, rather a spirit of power, love, and self-discipline" (2 Timothy 1:7). As a result, those

> " *God is always the answer to the power of fear and the enemy's attacks.* "

hurt in a dysfunctional family that lean on the Lord, can reason better, control the impact of their emotions, and decide differently and most honorably.

A PERSONAL EXAMPLE OF SATAN'S POWER IN FAMILIES

The Lord does send the right people and resources to those suffering with family issues when we ask HIM for it. I remember a time in my early ministry when our young daughter was filled with fear because I was traveling to another state for a conference. Her first fear that her dad might crash in an airplane was followed by additional anxious thoughts. Before long, her little mind was imagining each day that I might not be alive when she came home from school. No matter what we said to her or how we tried to comfort her, that negative imagination led to school phobia. Medical checkups and prescribed medicine would not stop her lack of sleep and many tears when she was to be separated from her parents. We prayed a lot.

Then we found special reading material from Focus on the Family on that subject that assured her that Jesus would guard her parents and soon give her peace to trust Him. Then a kind, personal letter to her from Doctor Dobson went a long way in helping her overcome those fears. Support from gracious teachers and administrators in the middle school of our city, and gradual half days of returning to school enabled Rebekah to work her way to a comfortable level of our being away from her. Bettie and I saw this serious psychological issue as a spiritual attack on our family and a real test for our ministry. Thankfully, our Savior and Lord brought all of us through that difficult year.

The true believer does have a power different from non-believers. The Holy Spirit inside works with our spirit to enable us to think clearly, understand the truth, and guide us to the steps we should take (see John 16:13). As hymn writer Clara H Scott says in her famous hymn, *Open My Eyes that I Might See.*

Open my eyes that I might see glimpses of truth Thou hast for me.
Place in my hands the wonderful key that shall unclasp and set me free.
Silently now I wait for Thee, ready my God, Thy will to see.
Open my eyes, illumine me, spirit divine!

These truths we should share with our counselees. For no matter what they have gone through, God wants to give them "glimpses of truth" through your words. In future chapters I will show you just how the Mighty Counselor, the Holy Spirit, will "open their eyes." "(He) will teach you all things and will remind you of everything I have said" (John 14:26).

God's Word is "the wonderful key" that will set the victim of bitterness and anger free. *As we graciously point out what Satan has done to them and their parents,* God will open the eyes of many with whom we work. Their eyes will be "illumined by the Spirit Divine." His will can become clear. *It's time for us to earn their trust so we can "unclasp" their emotional dungeon of despair.*

Despite the failings of our nation and the work the devil is doing in our communities, God is greater! *We can have the tools now to charge the gates of hell (Matthew 16:18-19), and with God's Spirit leading us, we can truly help our clients to be healed spiritually and emotionally from Satan's strong fiery darts.* Jesus said to the disciples "greater things than this will you do" (John 14:12-13). Mature and committed believers can decide to love, believe, and ask Him for strength to do His work. *Christ will give us His power to help hurting people overcome the devil's efforts!*

Chapter 6

GOD'S GRACE FOR PERSONAL WORTH

With everything the Enemy throws against the human race, God has provided and promised us HIS grace. Grace is a miracle that only HE can make happen. The purpose is to show us HIS Love. *When leaders in the family are unstable in their reasoning and designing, our merciful Lord wants to show us how to rebuild the lives of each person in that crooked and collapsing household.* The devil and his workers try hard to ruin the foundation of the family.

In Matthew 7:24-27 the writer compares the stories of two houses, one built on the rock and the other on the sand. Regarding the second house it is said, "When the rain fell and the floods came, and the winds blew and beat against that house, great was the fall of it!" (paraphrase of v. 27). That is a metaphor that might well apply to dysfunctional families that fail. But in Jesus there is hope to rebuild such families.

By the great tools of HIS Word Jesus gives the power now to re-build and re-establish any family who has fallen from life's adverse winds. Just as there are many ways that qualified workers can remodel a damaged physical structure and turn it into a strong and comfortable place for kids to be raised, there are likewise many ways God can rebuild the relational structure of a dilapidated household. It takes time and piece-by-piece labor to remodel a neglected, once beautiful dwelling. So, it also takes time and painstaking plans and corrections to provide a stronger and more functional living space in the hearts and minds of weather-beaten people. This idea of putting things back together is the mindset I had for the front cover of this book - the broken house with a weather-caused (but heart-shaped) hole in its front. The pieces lying on the shelf exemplify the remodeling work that God is yet to accomplish in such a dysfunctional household!

New blueprints are needed to remodel the family. Jesus can be the foundation for a new and loving house. The wise man can build his house on that rock (Matthew 7:24). Throwing out the faded and rotten

> "*New blueprints are needed to remodel the family.*"

materials of the past will set the family back on more solid ground.

To aid in this remodeling of a family, let us see how an understanding of boundaries can rebuild the weak spots that a strong-willed parent may have established in the household, because he or she thought that their young kids needed to be better than they appear – to them.

WRONG BUILDING MATERIALS TO USE

Perhaps a dad places too much emphasis on the athletic ability of one child above the talents or personalities of the other children. This builds jealousy, the "Jacob-Joseph syndrome" of Genesis 37. Jacob the father of 12 sons noticeably loved Joseph more because he was the first child of his favored wife, Rachel who had died. The things he did for Joseph were so plentiful that it caused the rest of the boys to be extremely jealous and full of hatred. Siblings become angry today, as well, when a parent shows favoritism. It becomes obvious with the family when a parent prefers one child over the others. Often the dad or mom does not see their partiality. Such favoritism could be because the father wants to live out his boyhood dreams of being a gifted athlete that he was unable to fulfill himself. His concealed psychological plan is to regain his pride. In his mind that is far from abuse or neglect.

As a result, the rest of the family may suffer a lack of attention while dad insists on taking his prodigy as far into stardom as he can rise with him. Even though the neglected family members will pull together and root for this exciting run, there is usually a hidden jealousy that is kept under wraps—for a while. The issue then is the father's selfish, strong, silent need to develop better self-esteem for himself. Dad does not realize his macho-man controlling way is building himself, not his family. It is vain and sinful.

Another example might be a mom allowing her daughters to grow up too fast. She might encourage them to use too much make-up and hair and nail arrangements that are an embarrassment to their chagrined father. This is the danger warned by New Testament authors about "pride and modesty" (see 1 Timothy 2:9; 1 Peter 3:3-4). Mom's conforming and controlling view pushes her daughters to be overly noticed by others, patterning them to be just like Mom was when she was young. Her plan is for her girls to be attractive and to draw the boys' attention. That lifestyle, however, is not what God intended for girls. Rather it should be closer to what Peter describes as "pure, reverent, gentle, and a quiet spirit." Thus, it may be very difficult for them to find who they really are as young adults because of how they were pushed and even brainwashed to be what Mom wanted them to be.

A girl persuaded in such a way might become discontented and feel unfulfilled. Or she may be influenced to try to be someone that she really is not. It may take her a long time to find satisfaction and peace because she was held back mentally and emotionally by being forced into mother's proper child.

But then, a second daughter might enjoy the attention at a young age. Now Mom is using a flimsy worldly philosophy that thrills her inside; but unfortunately, is keeping the daughter immature. Often a result is that she gives in too quickly to the persuasive flirtation of a selfish young man who feels similarly. Sexual temptation often becomes too strong for them. So, from poor training, this daughter learns to use her appearance to obtain what she really does not need in her young unguarded heart and life.

A third dysfunctional set-up might involve a parent who is far too strict in discipline regarding social issues while the spouse is uncomfortable with such rigidity. When one adult insists on perfection or nearly faultless obedience, arguments will likely ensue because mom and dad cannot agree on the right way to raise and correct their children. So, the kids are put in uncomfortable positions, not knowing whether to favor one parent or to use the other.

This controlling situation produces chaos and confusion, resulting in unhappy children. These adults should consider the instruction of the Apostle Paul, "Fathers, do not provoke your children to anger, but bring them up in the discipline and instruction of the Lord" (Ephesians 6:4 NLT). It is wrong and foolish for parents to let their own pride produce bitter children. It would be far better to prayerfully compromise on what is permissible than to present a divided front.

BOUNDARIES

With these examples we need to be reminded of the definition of dysfunction from chapter 1: **a household where harmony between the members is lost, and relationships are distant, critical, and disturbing (even dangerous); and will likely stay that way!** Relationship problems just described occur in these homes and keep them from experiencing emotionally healthy environments.

One person's strong opinion, overreach, argumentative attitudes, or disruptive behavior can make things uneasy and unworkable in the home. These are the strong winds and sudden floods that weaken and soon break the house apart. In each of the above family situations there is a lack of understanding of God-given human boundaries. Each person is responsible for his or her own actions; yet young people need to be told and shown what attitude is best and what actions are expected of them. Children need to be taught early to understand the gracious rules in the house; as well as how to take responsibility even regarding personal property. These important parameters, when taught with love and care, will help the young individual grow to be a mature adult.

Too often however, when parents hold on to, manipulate, or make demands of their kids, they break down inborn privacy fences of the mind. These innate strengths of the brain help children discover their identity—who they are and why they are unique. But overbearing parents will move into and take over some mental-spiritual property that rightly belongs to the developing child. The three controlling parents described above are over-stepping their roles.

Henry Cloud and John Townsend write in their masterpiece, **Boundaries,**

> In the hidden spiritual world, boundaries are just as real as physical property lines, but often harder to see. We must recognize intangible boundaries as an ever-present reality that can increase our love and save our life. They define our soul and help us guard and maintain it.[16]

Willing parents looking for help need to learn about and safeguard these invisible mental and spiritual areas. This is the first step in seeing God's grace make a family of Flawed Parents become healthy and strong – learning about and setting up family boundaries!

The aggressive father can go too far in forcing the athletic son to be what he wants him to be. The young man needs to decide for himself how far he wants to go in competition. Encourage, dream? Yes. Demand or demean? No. Sooner or later the boy needs his own space and permission to say what he wants to do.

The worldly mother pushes into her daughters' minds a striving to become popular and charming. Where is there an opportunity for the daughter to decide? Likewise, the perfectionist dad does not allow his children to discover or express the freedom to make their own choices. How will they learn from their own mistakes?

---

[16] Henry Cloud, John Townsend, *Boundaries*, Zondervan Publishing House, Grand Rapids, MI, 2004, 35.

> " *The spirit of discovery and learning...*
> *is often gone from their heart after they*
> *leave the house.* "

Each one of these strong-willed adults, though doing this in love, misunderstands the boundaries necessary for their children to mature and be alert to God. This important principle of allowing enough independence for them to discover their own potential is missed by the child growing up in these stressful homes. The spirit of discovery and learning how to use their God-given talents is often gone from their heart after they leave the house. These kinds of Controlling parents are unwittingly trampling on the "wellspring of life" rather than permitting their child to be able to "guard their heart" in the future. Solomon says proper wisdom from selfless and caring adults of the home are life and health to their children. (Proverbs 4:22, 23) We will see this again in chapter 10 on the "Functional Family."

Understanding and developing boundaries is very important for flawed parents to discover. Part of God's grace is allowing HIS children to find ways to demonstrate HIS characteristics. Christian parents must allow the Holy Spirit to work out the fruit of the spirit in their own lives. To want the best for our offspring is built into the adult soul. *We must help our adult clients to see the great need for balance between guiding their future and encouraging them to find their place in life. Setting boundaries is that important first step in helping our kids discover God's will and to pursue HIS calling.*

The writer of Proverbs says it well in his beginning chapters.

My Son, if you receive my words and treasure my commands within you . . . then you will understand the fear of the Lord, and find the knowledge of God, 2:1, 5.

Discretion will preserve you, understanding will keep you, to deliver you from the way of evil, 2:11-12.

Let not mercy and truth forsake you . . . Write them on the tablet of your heart. And so find favor and high esteem in the sight of God and man, 3:3-4. (NKJV)

Reader, can you help the older adult children you counsel to accept the importance of allowing the Lord to show them how to do what is best for their kids whether saved or not? Some homes collapse because of overly striving (Perpetuator) adults. They also miss the boundaries.

THE WINDS OF LIFE AND A CHAOTIC FLAWED PARENT

But then there are dysfunctional families where the home falls because the winds and floods of life beat down on the weaker parental personalities. Let me tell you a story of how a "Chaotic Mom" almost destroyed her daughter until the Lord intervened. This testimony will show us the second step in using the grace of God to raise wholesome and healthy children. Overcoming a poor self-image is very important to help kids discover just who they are, and what their Maker had in mind with the talents and future spiritual gifts they have been given. Finding value and worth will also equip them to build positive relationships with people who come into their lives.

The pastor of a neighboring church in conversation about self-esteem suggested I read Robert McGee's book, *The Search for Significance*. I have already used reference to it before here. This Pastor explained how this material had helped him work with a young lady who felt inferior, hopeless, and isolated from others. Dr. McGee calls this "shame" which was brought on by the negative influence of her melancholy mother. He writes that shame is one of the false belief systems that children of dysfunction are forced to endure.[17]

This counselee's mother was a "Chaotic Parent" with a lackadaisical and disorganized attitude. It was an attempt to make life easy, less stressful, and even mostly comfortable for herself and her only child. But instead, she caused her teenager to be undisciplined, unkempt, and even unattractive. Mom was unconcerned at how outsiders viewed her daughter. She allowed her to develop a lazy, uncaring attitude about schoolwork, school friends, or even what to achieve after graduation.

Mom's moody, uncertain personality had created a private, insecure person with little ambition and no interest in becoming who she was meant to be. With an extremely laid-back lifestyle, Mom had not only influenced daughter to become sullen and very shy, but she also stole the inborn desire to find herself and discover the reason she was born. There were no boundaries kept here. This child did not know her identity nor the potential God had placed within her mind and soul.

With poor self-worth and little control of her own feelings, Sara had just muddled through life, following everyone else's suggestions or persuasions; and now she found herself an empty adult. In her late twenties Sara was wondering what she had accomplished and why she was not married. She was wrestling with these thoughts since her own mother had just let her down again. Grandma did not want to help with her rambunctious, misbehaving two-year-old boy.

She does have to admit she has made a dysfunctional family for her young son, as her religious co-worker has graciously told her. She could

---

[17] Robert S. McGee, *The Search for Significance*, Rapha Publishing, Houston, TX, 1990, 41.

blame things on her often-absent mom or the dad she never met. For although Mother provided decent food, shelter, and clothing during her growing up years; there were never many compliments for positive accomplishments, nor much guidance to help make right decisions. Sara could not remember having help with homework or advice on girl teen drama at school. Perhaps that is why she was never popular or had more than one or two friends.

As she pondered over her difficulties and loneliness, she felt embarrassed that she had never broken away from the hold of her mother. This is an example of the "shame principle" that McGee describes in his book. Sara had developed a pessimistic outlook on life and now felt guilty for being so passive, withdrawn, and afraid of building helpful relationships. That could explain the horrific one-nightstand she had four years ago with a persuasive man who worked as an executive at their business. The two never dated afterward, as he was working his way up the corporate ladder, and she was unimportant to him, anyway. The man soon moved away, and Sarah never told him that she was pregnant.

Over the years she formed a pattern of being comfortable doing things by herself. She became a perfectionist at cleaning her kitchen and took solace in reading women's magazines and romance novels. Then she became an expert at filing papers and organizing her boss' office. Ironically, all these things were the opposite of what mom had done in their house.

There had never been any talk at home about her strengths or talents. She never had a chance to stretch her horizon. Mom did not have any hobbies. They were not involved in any social events, did not take trips to the shopping mall or movie theater together, and certainly never went to church. Because of the shame principle Mom never seemed positive or confident in herself. Without realizing it, she passed on the same fears and social resistance to her daughter.

Then Sara's new co-worker friend, seemingly out of nowhere, invited her to join an exciting Sunday morning worship service. This happy, positive single woman about her age seemed sincere, so Sara decided to do something different.

When they got to the church building, Susan helped Sara put her son in the toddler room; then they went into the auditorium to hear the Christian music and listen to the interesting pastor. The speaker used a book he called the Bible to show Sara that his God had a great interest in all people who were struggling to discover who they were. That morning for the first time, Sara began to feel that someone important valued her as a person. Perhaps it was time to get to know this Jesus, who the preacher said was so kind and loving and "full of grace."

During the next few weeks, life began to have a new meaning. Sara and Susan became good friends. She found she could open up and talk about her past. Sara became surprisingly comfortable in discussing her mistakes, and now she wished to be set free mentally from her embarrassment and grief. One Sunday she decided to find out if Jesus would forgive her, and if guilt could be taken away. Sara went forward at the altar call and felt free and light as air. She knew now that she could be a child of God, important to Him and accepted as a new person. She could live as a cleansed individual and serve her new Savior for the rest of her life. She now had the strong motivation to proudly love her son in a new way, as a precious gift from God. With her conversion she believed she had significance because the Lord knew and had loved her all along.

People in the congregation discipled Sara and helped her find her spiritual gifts. Now she is serving Christ at the church every Sunday morning as a greeter and is showing others how to connect with good Christian friends. Sara is growing closer to God through the Small Group she is attending. She has found several new friends and has learned how important it is to offer her own opinions with the rest of the Bible study group.

Mom has found Christ too and attends the same church. However, Teresa is not growing spiritually. She is not willing to change her habits and, unfortunately, is satisfied living a life without real purpose. Long ago, Sara's grandma had taken her own life as a young mother. And Teresa had been raised by adoptive parents who were never able to show her real love or that she was really wanted. So currently she still feels unloved even by God. For now, she remains unwilling to trust anyone or allow them to help her overcome her own poor self-image. In her mind, even Jesus cannot or will not help her. Although Sara and her friends continue to pray for Teresa, an alert Church Counselor needs to spend some time with Mom to work on shame, self-esteem, and God's overwhelming love!

So, this unhappy "Chaotic Mom" raised a chaotic daughter. Sara had lived a difficult and undisciplined life and would have raised her son in the same pattern. But Jesus intervened! HE brought her to understand she was very loved and important to HIM. As the Children's song goes, "God don't make no junk!"

The Deuteronomy 5:9 curse was broken through the evangelistic efforts of a good Christian friend. Susan was used by God to show Sara she was created with a special plan in mind. A poor self-image was

Satan's plan, and the Holy Spirit demolished that stronghold of feeling worthless.

Sara's example shows that the life of a hurt second-generation parent can be altered through the work of a strong caring associate. Sometimes this outsider will simply be a seed planter, so that others with evangelistic gifts or calling can be the ones that reach them. And *sometimes a willing church counselor can be the instrument that God uses to lift someone out of the pit of despair.* The two steps previously mentioned in this chapter will enable us to see God's grace rewrite the Blueprints to rebuild a dilapidated family. Again, they are *operating with good boundaries and strengthening their self-image!*

I have a heavy burden not only to see souls saved but also to watch them be built up to become mature Christians who demonstrate the power and glory of God. I am writing this book because I believe there are many people around us who are struggling with the past and therefore, are not living out their potential. Many of our friends at church long to be confident and peaceful believers. They are waiting for someone to show them God's grace to be set free of their deep regret of the past and their suffering remorse over a hideous childhood. *They need miracles of grace that God may well choose to work through You!*

And every church can have a ministry or individual leader who can help people find their peace and significance in life. God is waiting for us to act. "The eyes of the Lord are on the righteous, and His ears are open to their cry . . . The righteous cry out, and the Lord hears them, he delivers them from all their troubles" (Psalm 34:15,17).

UNIT III

POWER TO CHANGE THE FAMILY

Unit III

POWER TO CHANGE
THE FAMILY

Individual families take on the sinful influences of the parents. For the descendants to live as God intended, HE must break into the group and fill someone there with HIS overwhelming Love. Without the touch or drawing of the invisible Holy Spirit there would be no opportunity for people to live together in unity, humility, kindness, or positive direction. But we are all born with that much talked about sin nature that makes us selfish, proud, and greedy.

But it is the role of Dad and Mom to train the young ones to share things with others, and to be kind and generous toward siblings and little classmates. In daily life adults are automatically inclined to give children what is best, and to explain to them how to make lasting friends. In Chapter 7 I will point out that the LORD also can teach and show each family member how to be filled with HIS kind of sacrificial love as they relate to one another. No matter how chaotic or mean-spirited connections have or might become, the love that families need to operate with is supernatural. So, only a believer in a dysfunctional family can willingly allow the Holy Spirit to take over.

In this Unit I have sought to put myself in the place of the sufferers of Dysfunction. I view the aches and pains of the second-generation parent from a psychological angle to understand their often inability to patch-up or overlook the mistakes of the past. I will teach from Jesus' parable on forgiveness the significant impact that pardoning and forgiving can have on the rest of the family for decades.

Then Chapter 9 covers the need to be alert to all the tricky things that Satan shoots at even Christian families to mess up as many minds as possible. When an open person turns to God, he or she will find positive thoughts that will direct them to peace and inner strength. Spiritual power from the Holy Spirit will guide counselors to show parents how to pull down strongholds, and to restart the process of restoring and rebuilding their broken household!

Chapter 7

"AGAPE LOVE" WORKS

Love can take heartaches away. Love can build confidence in people. Love can restore relationships. Love can turn the world upside down. Love is what we all need. But as we have been saying throughout, LOVE is MISSING in Dysfunctional Families!

What if suddenly people learned how to love? What if forgiveness were expressed and people who mistrusted or were afraid of each other in a household were seen enjoying and seriously encouraging one another again? What if a father, who had berated and discouraged his son, suddenly decided to admit his wrong and apologized for the damage he had done years before. What if he began spending as much time as possible sincerely caring about his grandchildren? These two brief illustrations of change in the heart would be called miracles. I would also say they were the supernatural action of "Agape-Love."

We know that GOD is always working on the earth (John 5:17); and when asked by a believer, HE wants to answer prayer (see chapters

4 and 5) and perform miracles in broken families. So, why is love not given the chance to work in damaged relationships? Why is it so hard for an angry mother to begin to express heart-felt kindness to a rebellious, loud-mouthed son? Why can't a disappointed daughter overlook her busy dad's broken promise to attend her championship volleyball game? Why is it so difficult to love someone who lets you down or even betrays you? It is because our human nature can take only so much adjustment or alteration from what makes us happy. It takes supernatural strength to overcome the wrong that we suffer. As sinners, even though we are all born with a longing to be loved by someone, we have an inner defense mechanism that wants us to push away because of our fear of being severely hurt. It is just hard to trust someone who has clearly sinned against us whether on purpose or accidentally.

So, to avoid the full experience of emotional pain or grave disappointment, we put on a mask or façade to cover up how we really feel. Or perhaps we more often respond in anger with raised voice or threats of retaliation. Even though we have been told that two wrongs don't make a right, our wounded feelings take over. We often get into the habit of allowing our emotions to get out of control. Others in a similar situation might remain quiet and secretly plan ways to hurt the offending person. They foolishly believe that getting even will ease the pain.

To this type of "old self" reaction, Christ says, "In everything, do to others what you would have them do to you" (Matthew 7:12). Despite the wrong that has been committed, HE will give the believer the power to pardon and forgive, and then the desire to do right to that person who did him wrong. (See more detail on this point in the next chapter.) The true Christian can love more people than just his friends or kind neighbors. In Matthew 5:44 Jesus teaches that we are to pray for those

"The true Christian can love more people than just his friends or kind neighbors."

who injure us. When a Christian uses this spiritual weapon and prays for someone who is hard to love, usually God's Spirit will gradually change his or her now open heart.

Let us look again at some of the tenets of this book to see if we can figure out the tremendous help love would give. If flawed parents (*Originators*) would yield to a better way, second generation (*Perpetuators*) adults could then better forgive. This paves the way for their teens (*Inheritors*) to open their minds to new positive examples.

Love is a strong force that can overcome evil. In I Corinthians 13 the Apostle Paul says it does not envy, boast, or show pride (I Corinthians 13:4). So, if God's kind of love is expressed, hearts can be changed for real and for good. And "dysfunctional families" will write a new story.

The Greek word Paul uses for love is "*agape*." He is speaking about a sacrificial, unconditional, undeserved kind of affection or concern for another. It is <u>sacrificial</u> when the Christian determines to think less of himself and more of the person he is dealing with. It is <u>unconditional</u> in that she is led to give to someone's need without expecting any thanks or kindness in return. And agape is <u>undeserved</u> from the standpoint that the one being cared for doesn't have to prove his worth before the believer demonstrates a planned act of kindness.

This kind of miraculous love is surely needed in every family. Parents must sacrifice for their young ones. Children can do the same for parents without waiting for praise. And neither side should think they deserve or expect a goodwill gesture in return. So, we can apply agape love to both difficult parents and reactionary kids. Plus, sacrificial love can even be applied to someone who hasn't even arrived in the family yet!

LOVE FOR THE UNBORN

Studies by American gynecologists and pediatricians have proven that a baby in the womb can feel, touch, and smell by 8 to 10 weeks. The little guy or gal inside can sense its environment beyond the uterus through special neurons from mom in utero that attach to the baby's brain. Mother produces oxytocin, called the "love hormone" in the hypothalamus at the base of her brain. Then this chemical is released into the bloodstream by mom's pituitary gland. The main function of this hormone is to facilitate childbirth, and to produce positive feelings.

But the infant can recognize mom's stress when it is caused by bad health or difficult experiences with the father – because the love hormone stops reaching the blood stream during emotional stress. Plus, the unborn can experience a sense of security if things are at peace in Mommy's outside world. So, it is important that the mother sing, speak softly, or even casually exercise, to produce that "love hormone" as the Preborn is working his or her way out. The birth canal is a scary place, but with oxytocin swarming around, the baby can sense that there is more love on the other side! Then when the infant is placed on the mother's chest for cuddling and feeding, oxytocin is sent through the milk as well, to provide comfort to the newborn and via special capillaries to warm mom's chest. Our Lord biologically and routinely supplies love through the mother that the infant can notice.

Conversely, babies who are taken from their moms never experience this kind of love. Studies have shown that in hospitals or orphanages where the newborn is not held, spoken to with care, nor supplied with the love hormone - the children grow up nervous, unattached, or rejecting the many attempts of nurses or foster and adopting mothers to care or provide for them. As the baby matures to a toddler it develops a psychological sense that he/she is unworthy or unwanted![18] Love makes a difference!

LOVE WORKS WITH MOM AND DAD

Let us look at the impact that sacrificial love can have on the four types of flawed parents we've already exposed and studied. For the **Controlling** Dad who demands things his way and the **Conforming** Mom who manipulates things her way; Christ's love would take away their self-centeredness. The need to control others would be replaced with the desire to help the kids for their own benefit. They could become affectionate functional families as I describe them later in the next unit. So, if these two types of parents were saved and committed to purposefully growing in the Lord, over time their outlook would greatly change. Remember, 2 Corinthians 5:17 teaches that the person who is in Christ is a new creation. For him the old has gone, the new has come. Others in the home would notice this difference and would be pleased at this alteration from the way the changed person now treats the younger ones in the family. Soon siblings would unexpectedly begin to admire this adult for the good gestures that are being demonstrated.

---

[18] Speaker Stacey Gagnon, Trauma Conference by Lost Sparrows, Warsaw, IN, September 2023

For the **Chaotic** Dad who wants little responsibility and the **Coddling** Mom who wants little stress in the house, agape love would dissipate their fear of being involved personally with their children. Many of these parents would change their grown kids' and grandkids' lives. When the Holy Spirit would move in the hearts of these two types of adults, God would also work on softening the hearts of their off-spring. What the Apostle John says about "perfect love" in his first letter (4:18) could become real in these once dysfunctional families. The fear or hesitancy to open up and get involved with their young would slowly go away. The better love of wanting to find ways to guide them to do what God wants would become foremost in the minds of mom and dad. These two types of more passive parents could be empowered by God's Spirit (1 John 4:13) to live in love because they would be submitting to HIS Word. They then become confident in a perfect love (agape) that pushes them to honestly admire their Lord and seriously care about their kids, HIS way!

Changing hearts in cruel or distant parents would be miraculous. And as the Holy Spirit works on them to repent for all the harm they had previously caused, even the most bitter child would be able to see the difference. The other siblings, who would want to give the flawed parent a second chance, could then work on a more resistant brother or sister. *This kind of demonstration of amazing power, doubtless, is God's plan for the family you are working with. Why not believe it is possible over time by what the Lord is doing with them through you?* When amazing Adonai (Lord) intervenes with the first-generation parents, the world of the dysfunctional family can certainly be turned "right-side-up".

Let me say here that a changed heart would also find reason to treat the spouse much better. When the Gospel of Grace grabs the soul of one parent, the other is sanctified through the believing mate (I Corinthians 7:14). I believe Paul means that God's Spirit pours HIS attention onto the nonbeliever in such a way that HE will answer the prayers of the humble and maturing saved one. The Christ-like born again parent/mate will show a concerned and co-opting spirit toward the resistant one. Agape love in the child of God will initiate a desire to treat the unspiritual adult with greater respect and more grace and kindness. This will often gradually open eyes and alert the unsaved one to God's clearer supernatural work.

I will never forget a testimony I witnessed years ago. A gruff alcoholic who worked in a paper mill and owned a beer joint got radically saved one day. His wife had attended church and prayed for ten years for her husband to accept Christ and change. She endured some terrible experiences in an alcohol-run, dysfunctional family with two precious daughters because she believed the Loving Lord would answer her prayer. The Holy Spirit drastically got hold of this man. He changed so much that he became a great soul winner for the church. He told many of his fellow factory workers that he knew that Jesus had died for his sin and shared about the wonderful things God was doing in his life. Galen also became a leader in the bus ministry of his church and graciously went into several homes in the area on Sunday mornings to bring children to church even before their parents were saved.

This is proof of the verse in James 5:16 that says, "The prayer of a righteous person is powerful and effective." Our God wants to show HIS power and love in a dysfunctional home, and when godly people are willing instruments of that miraculous spiritual force, nothing is too difficult for HIM!

AGAPE IN THE MARRIAGE MAKES A DIFFERENCE

This brings me back to another one of the main principles weaved throughout this book. *Too many couples have lost sight of the point that dads and moms must work more sincerely at loving each other and must strive more earnestly to pass on sacrificial love to their precious children.* Sincere love of each other is what I want to discuss now.

Many homes have become dysfunctional because husband and wife have lost their original attraction for each other and have forgotten their first commitment in those good vows they recited once in God's presence. By now they have thrown away their willingness to continue in unconditional love toward one another. The flame of romance has been put out, and the spark to keep giving what their sweetheart needs has dwindled or died. The promise to always support one another's good ambitions has been stolen from their tired and beat down minds - through too many conflicts, unkind words, and sudden changes of plans. The primary reason they do not work together and refuse to treat the kids right is that they "don't love each other anymore." They both feel betrayed.

But the real problem, as Counselor Gary Collins says, is self-centered sin. It is the refusal to stop blaming each other for their issues and to refuse to get help for compromising and better understanding the role that each person plays in the conflicts. When they just cover up their mistakes and try to deny their own part in the problem, the "sin that needs to be confronted, confessed, and then followed up with changed behavior," never happens.[19] If more adults would realize their children are destined to suffer more than children of forgiving

---

[19] Gary R. Collins, *Family Shock*, Carol Stream, IL, Tyndale House, 1995, 55-57

marriages, perhaps they would work harder at the important need to pardon and forgive as is described in chapter 8.

Surveys and professional counselors report that children of divorced parents are more likely to feel insecure, experience depression, and live with low self-esteem. They develop anxiety about future relationships, have little ability to trust people, and are more vulnerable to stress.[20]

The biblical solutions addressed in Chapter 9 on strongholds and Chapter 11 on peace could give the hurting second-generation adults more reason to pursue reconciliation in their own marriage. Then will come a reason to start over with a greater desire to have a healthy, even happy family from there on. In addition to advice on dysfunction, many people need a marriage counselor. If you cannot help with this second role, why not include another advisor to complement or substitute for you in working with the couple for a while.

So, agape love can most often bring a different outcome in crippled families. Remember, we are talking sacrifice. It is not "I have the right to demand, such and such." It is "I have the responsibility under God and my promise at our wedding to give my best to you." It is not "Here's how I feel toward you." Rather what counts is "This is what God wants me to do for you." *We should not allow people to live by fickle feelings. We should try to motivate those who listen to us to live by God's Word and their own promises. Some might say to you, "I can't get my love back." But I am suggesting you say to them, "How much are you willing to give up of yourself to honor and obey the merciful God?"* If you submit to HIM, HE can recreate love in your heart and in your mate's. Ephesians 3:20 says, "Now to him who is able to do immeasurably more than all we ask

---

[20] Ibid, 218

> " *If you submit to HIM,*
> *HE can recreate love in your heart*
> *and in your mate's.* "

or imagine, according to his power that is at work in us." Any Christian couple can believe and trust this promise.

LOVE WORKS FOR THE KIDS, TOO

Then there is the prescription for young kids, teenagers, and older children. *Guide them through the types of roles kids play* that we discussed earlier (scapegoat, mascot, loner, and hero; see chapter 1). *Explaining these roles might help the kids to be more open to see why and how they missed proper love. So as grown children they would be more apt to consider the work their LORD wants to do for them.* The effect of Agape on these four kinds of wounded children is explained more fully under the next sub-title section, pages 121–123.

Some kids could become more bitter; God may have to push harder on them after your original approach. But most of the second generation will be grateful for the new information. As they think about past unkind acts or words, they will recognize that God was not allowed by the parents to work in the family at that time. But *HE is ready to greatly alter things now. If these Perpetuators are ready to submit to HIM and HIS plan for their lives, good relationships can be rebuilt.* Here's where God's words to Israel might well be applied to families today: "I know the plans

I have for you, declares the Lord, plans to prosper you and not harm you (anymore), plans to give you hope and a future" (Jeremiah 29:11).

When teens or young adults are saved, they will look hard at their own sinful actions and statements. God's Spirit will soften them. They will start to think, "what if I would have done this instead of that"? The hurt or angry 15–25 year-old will be Spirit-led to ASK, SEEK, and KNOCK (Matthew 7:7). Ask the Lord in faith for answers, seek HIS presence through Scripture, and knock by stepping forward with HIS insight in their mind. The main points of my next chapter on forgiveness will begin to weigh on them heavily. Since they now have Christ working on their spirit, they will, in most cases, come to the place where they will really want to make things right - HIS timing, of course. All this is Agape love.

When I accepted Christ at age 22, one of the important things I did was to tell my mother that I no longer had hard feelings toward her for the role she played in my parents' divorce. She knew I was the peacemaker personality (Scapegoat) and admired me for that. She recognized that my heart had softened more. So, at that time she felt she could express a heartfelt apology to me. I went out on a bold limb and dared to share that if she and Dad had gone to the Lord and got marriage counseling back then, the fighting and separating would not have occurred. Mom acknowledged that, stating that she did not know Jesus personally then. She responded humbly and graciously, "But Rick, you know that my whole second family (of four more children) would not have been born had I stayed with your dad".

I realized it was wrong and unprofessional for me to think I know better in all situations. To try to change someone's past is impossible! Thus, I became thankful again for all the blessings God had given to both families. Over the years the Lord had allowed me to have three important half-sisters and one committed half-brother. They are special and I love them too.

After pondering this conversation, I concluded that it was ridiculous for me to judge my mother's sin or try to be God. I again needed to settle for the truth that it is difficult enough to acknowledge and overcome my own sin. My own wounds as a second-generation person of dysfunction could be overcome, if I allowed Christ to work on changing and molding me into the person God wanted me to be. Then I could let HIM work on my mom, my sister, and Mom's other family as HE saw fit. A counselor can do only so much. And when it is close and personal and with blood relatives, our impact may be even less. Remember Jesus said, "No prophet is accepted in his hometown" (Luke 4:24). And advice from a seeming know-it-all pastor/counselor is usually not welcomed from wounded brothers and sisters still dealing with their own dysfunctional struggles.

However, love is mightier than sin. And God's love works in and through HIS children to conquer sin. After that significant conversation, I understood that I could, with God's help, show my love to my mother in all kinds of special and personal ways in the months and years to come. I would never want to judge her again. That would enable her to relax with me, and for us to build a solid relationship together.

AGAPE AND UNDERSTANDING FOR THE FOUR ROLE-PLAYING KIDS

Most born again **Scapegoat** children (like me) who try so hard to fix the issues in the average dysfunctional home will begin to see the necessity of letting GOD work things out in HIS schedule. And this person will suddenly come to realize they did not have the supernatural help previously to change mom or dad. *But prayer with the Scapegoat, and our living and explaining Scripture to them can gradually be used to make them more sensitive to doing things differently and better.* Allowing GOD's agape love to work through this personality now will help to convince the rest of the family that Jesus is real and that HE really wants all of them to be part of HIS family.

When **Mascot** or clown is saved, he will look at his own mistakes in the past humorously and comment that he/she was too dumb and silly to understand that trials were meant to make them stronger. Mature believers do not deny struggles or push them away unsettled. But in the Lord's timing HE will use this child to remind everyone of the futility of selfishness, jealousy, greed, and name-calling. And as the Lord often works, it is the mascot in the family that catches the heavenly hints. Then he must listen to HIM from now on. For it is never too late to see that the Almighty has a wonderful plan for each of their lives.

As for the **Loner**, when convinced of God's love, he will want it immensely. He or she will desire to be swallowed up in the blanket of God's care and power. This person will take to heart the promises in Psalms to be covered by and hidden in "the shadow of HIS wings" (17:8, NIV). He will daily find refuge (protection and strength) and rest (assurance that he is important to the Creator) in the shadow of God's Hand (Isaiah 51:16). There will be no more fear. He will understand better than the rest of us how I John 4:18 works: There is no fear in love. Perfect love drives out fear because fear has to do with punishment. He is the one who was still living in his own world, because he was secretly afraid someone in the family would punish or embarrass him for one of his shortcomings, which he has overblown in his mind. So, when this person is saved, he or she is very much set free. The Scripture in Romans

8:1 will come alive to him. There will no longer be even one condemnation because he is in Christ. He may be so excited that he will forget shyness and probably want to tell everyone the difference God's love has made in his mind and heart. *We counselors and pastors must surely give hope and freedom to the Loners we know.*

Last is the **Hero**. He or she, you remember, has lost any desire to love the parent who hurt him. So, to feel sorry for them or to pardon them for their sin is very difficult. But if this role-player were to focus on Christ's sacrifice and HIS attitude of humility, things would look different. The problem with heroes is that they have decided that amid the chaos in the family, they do not deserve nor should accept the mistreatment. In dealing with the harm or disappointment, they have determined it is better to look out for themselves. More than being concerned about others, life has become mainly about them. But in Philippians 2 Paul teaches us that Jesus willingly lived in humility amidst cruelty. God's Son left the glories of Heaven to live among the abuse and oppression that sinful adults would exert upon HIM. In verse 3 Paul says we should not focus on our own hurts and misery but recognize that maltreatment was an experience that God wanted us to go through. Countless others have undergone similar letdowns and crushed hopes in this world. Why should this hero be above that?

Paul explains that it is better in the long run to obey Christ and put up with the pain than to fight back and demand a more favorable recourse. And Peter in his first letter shares that a true believer will honor Jesus more by accepting unfair suffering when he or she is in the right. Christ, our example, did not retaliate or make threats but entrusted Himself into God's hand and HIS will (I Peter 2:20-23). *So again, we pastors should seek to help the hero that comes to our office to accept Christ as personal Savior so he or she will be able to comprehend or take on this kind of thinking. Perhaps then the wounded hero will understand that it was God's purpose for him to suffer* (v. 21, NASB).

Only agape love will alter the heart of this believing servant. It usually takes time and much study of the Bible to sift those enduring thoughts through one's soul. Although the hero certainly did not deserve his dysfunctional parent, neither did he deserve God's unconditional love. We do not work to be worthy of Jesus' love. It comes because in faith we believe and receive it. That's just who God is. And HE, the Almighty Lover, wants us to experience agape when we need it most.

We should also teach our clients that they should not keep to themselves what the Master desires the true believer to pass on to many others who have suffered as much or worse than they have. When a grown or mature child of dysfunction comes to understand God's great grace extended to them, the Holy Spirit will prod them to become ambassadors for Christ." Paul says in 2 Corinthians 5:18-20 that when we have become HIS Children we are given "the ministry of reconciliation." God intends on making His appeal for souls through us. The hero, in particular, has a great message to deliver. He has found his true worth by giving his pride away and submitting to the real loving Father.

> "*We do not work to be worthy of Jesus' love, in faith we believe and receive it.*"

MORE ON UNCONDITIONAL LOVE

The Apostle John also strongly conveys in his first letter that since God lives in us, HIS love is made complete in us. That is shown when we offer sacrificial love to others, especially those who are not kind to us. "Dear friends, since God so loved us, we also ought to love one another" (I John 4:11).

The Hero especially needs to practice this agape love. All the siblings *must be given the opportunity through us as the helpers, to demonstrate real love to family members no matter their age or their wrongdoing.*

Agape love is beyond our ability to comprehend. It is God (I John 4:8); and HE is infinite. HE is more than we are able to explain or to reason through. We are finite, our own capacity to understand sacrifice will eventually run out or dry up. But the Almighty, like HIS greatest characteristic of LOVE, is without any limits. There is no one HE cannot love and no problem HE cannot solve. Despite our terrible sin, Jesus came to pardon the vilest deed or the most wicked thought. It is up to everyone to want and to believe in that kind of infinite tender affection. Be filled with the spirit (Ephesians 5:18). This leads to submission to other family members too (5:21).

Now before we leave the important subject of agape love, we must revisit the problems that flawed parents cause. If they would allow agape love to work on their hearts, they could live with balance. That would be between what their personalities force them to do, and what God intends for them. Although their flaws cause them to either control or push away their children, these traits can be turned into powerful ways to demonstrate God's love.

In reading a booklet about addictions, and the reason why people cling to them so strongly, I realized that the four C's (Flawed Parents) that June Hunt describes and Living Free supports, can be considered addictions too. A pamphlet I found by RBC Ministries suggests that one reason people find it hard to give up habits is because of the "pursuit of power." "Addictions provide an illusion of control. They are like private magic carpets that transport us into a world where we seem to be in charge. They provide a predictable way of changing how we feel about ourselves and others."[21]

In thinking about the Controller, we note that he is very comfortable at being in charge of how things go at his house. And he wants it to stay that way. No matter who he hurts or when it happens, this "illusion of control" is that everyone else must serve his whims.

The Conforming parent feels so much better when the family automatically follows his or her wishes on a regular basis. This is her "magic carpet" ride to peace and satisfaction. This form of control provides a predictable way for things to roll.

Now the infusion of unconditional love (agape) means treating the children with what is best for their benefit without expecting anything in return. This way of living for the kids would break the "prediction of control" of these addictive-like parents. Mom and dad would be loving their offspring for the benefit and comfort of their kids, not themselves. With the Holy Spirit filling their minds with agape, there would be little selfishness and less chance of bad predictable moments to expect. *Think of how much stronger the family would be working together. Counseling on this kind of sacrificial love could really turn the situation around.*

---

[21] Quoted expressions here are from Tim Jackson and Jeff Olson, "When We Just Can't Stop," RBC Ministries, Grand Rapids, MI, 2011, 8-9.

And then the Coddling adults who want to let the kids do whatever they wish are in the comfortable habit of doing their own thing. They can be lolled into an emotional high of little responsibility that they long for most of their day. But often the child will mess something up by making a wrong or selfish choice. Now reality hits mom or dad. But they are not prepared for the sudden change or bad news, so clamor and confusion take over. They never seem to be ready for mishaps, and they rather live and work toward the sluggish mode of being in their own private world.

There is also the similarly broken parent that avoids as much responsibility as possible by providing all the gimmicks and gadgets to the children. This is so he or she can be left alone. But the Chaotic Parent's addiction is to laziness or pleasurable habits of his own. The Coddler cares about what the kids are doing but wants them to satisfy their own whims and desires. The Chaotic adult tries to quickly return to his or her game or hobby or out-of-the-house activity, which he thinks he earned the right to. Unfortunately, this adult is so entrapped by his unique avocation that he might forget about the kids for hours.

But when and if these two types of flawed parents would be confronted by a gracious counselor-pastor, they would often be pricked in their conscience or convicted in their soul if a true Christian. Then they could put aside their old way or habit and focus on the needs of their offspring. This is how the Holy Spirit works. Here messages, verses, or good illustrations of God's mercy and grace will usually stir the weaker parents to get away from their selfish daydreaming or greedy time-consuming activities. Positive teaching on Agape love could motivate them to change as discussed earlier on page 111. And the thrill of the Counselor's heart is to see lives and families altered for lasting good. This then will bring a desire to share with passion that God's Word brought change that made parents personally stronger and their families much healthier. "The God-breathed Scripture is useful for teaching, correcting, and training in what is right so that the people of God can be equipped for every good need that comes along in life (2 Timothy 3:16-17, my paraphrase).

Love makes a big difference. Love is the greatest of all human traits. Love covers a multitude of sins (I Peter 4:8). Love causes us to serve. Love surpasses and fills all knowledge. Love builds up and grows up

> " *The thrill of the counselor's heart is to see lives and families altered for lasting good* "

families. Love unites good people. Love comes from God! *We can do this! It does not have to be missing in Dysfunctional Families.*

CHART OF DIFFERENCE WE CAN MAKE

	CONTROLLING Bossy	CONFORMING Too orderly
CONSEQUENCE TO FAMILY	Fear, insecurity Fights among kids No trust, no joy Rebel versus parents	Compliance to help parents Resentment for their best Parent considered weak Parent becomes codependent

COUNSELING HELP	Created with leadership gifts Your parents wrong, learn truth God's plan for you-different and better. Trust Him	Organization is good Be less selfish Try to understand a kid's personality and needs Seek God's will first – above your own
RESULT HOPED FOR	Agape love – changed attitude Lessen pride, forgive them Submit to the Lord Let God show how to lead family	Agape love – think sacrificially Allowing God to develop kids His way Kids will notice change Praise God and ad- mire parents More harmony

	CODDLING Too giving	CHAOTIC Careless
CONSEQUENCE TO FAMILY	Kids enjoy material things Always want more Kids may be- come demanding Parents lose control Don't see kids' real needs	Children become careless and self- centered Only surface relationships Over-emphasis on body beauty
COUNSELING HELP	Peace important, but kids must give and cooperate also Parent set roles and rules for each person Show worship of God; not things	Think less of self, more of others God gives par- ent responsibility Be careful that parent's unhappiness not passed on to own kids
RESULT HOPED FOR	Agape love – want to be involved with kid's lives, hear their stories Kids come to parents for advice, not things God brings unforced peace and harmony	Agape love – want to see kids succeed more than themselves Morals demonstrated for kids Parents think better of themselves Use money wisely

This chart goes down vertically. We start with the difficult experiences that the Flawed Parent causes because of their negative traits. Then the 2nd step is the direction where the Counselor would lead the harmful parent to consider change. Step 3 then is the result we would hope God would bring to pass with our efforts to open the eyes of the wrongful Perpetuator Mom or Dad. For instance, the 4th Flawed Parent is Chaotic or undiscipline, usually selfish and even lazy. He/she will cause their children to be careless and self-centered. The Counselor would then encourage him with descriptions of Agape so he could think less of himself and more of others – his children. The Chaotic Parent will develop an honest desire for their children to be happier and more successful than they are/were. Morals and wise use of money and time would become more important; and be earnestly taught to their children.

Chapter 8

THE POWER
OF FORGIVENESS

We will look now at the work of the Holy Spirit from the perspective of young adults raising small children while still dealing with unsettled issues of dysfunction between them and their parents. If these second-generation family leaders have not become Christians yet, their view of life will be selfish and worldly as previously described in chapters 3 and 4. It will be very difficult for them to forget their actual mistreatment when they were young. And, as mentioned in chapter 1, they will be unaware that they are raising their kids very similarly to how they were treated. Dysfunction is generational and broken people make broken people. So, is there a key or two that can stop the hurt from repeating itself? We need to look at the bitterness that lingers from a damaged past.

I believe the best way to study how to overcome past anger or bitterness is to look closely at the Hero child who was formed in a broken home. You will remember that this personality, usually choleric (independent-minded and determined), will resist being pushed around, and would much rather leave the house than try to fix it. The reason for his resistance is not only because he feels he doesn't deserve his mistreatment (previous chapter) but that he or she is angry with the parent who will not consider his feelings or thoughts. In addition, because he is normally a more positive and creative person, the other siblings either hesitate to support him or they outright oppose his ideas and clever plans to retaliate against the dysfunctional parent. As a result, this selfish problem-solver either quits trying and fights alone or he makes a bad scene and walks out the door with his suitcase.

Until this grown and sour child can get over the wounds of childhood, she will hold her unreasonable parents responsible for her deep-down bitterness. This anguish will gradually eat away at her inside and then burst at a breaking point when least expected. The emotional outbursts will embarrass almost everyone, even relatives that are not responsible for or are unaware of the dysfunction. A public scene will create more separation between this young Hero parent and the grandparent for months or years to come.

The older folks don't understand the angst and have conveniently forgotten the sinful role they played in emotionally injuring this grown child of theirs. This was Jeff's problem in my opening story. Thinking his mistakes were forgiven by God meant to him that they should also be forgiven by his youngest boy, the Hero. Dad never asked Jack any personal questions, such as how he felt about his father or what might be bothering him. In fact, in Jeff's mind, this son was rebellious, disrespectful to his dad, and clearly disobeying God's fifth commandment to honor his father and mother. Blinded to the offensive and severe ways he had pushed his son away; Jeff felt the clashes they were having now were always Jack's doing.

But this control-minded fourth child could never reason with his always-right father. Neither adult could admit his wrongdoing. Neither over-bearing male could apologize to the other. Unless the Holy Spirit was allowed to penetrate their stubborn minds, they would live the rest of their lives far apart.

In this family's case, however, over a few years God enabled me to work with Jack concerning relational problems with a troubling girlfriend and then his own angry teenage daughter. During these additional trials which were mainly caused by his stubbornness, this second-generation son broke down and asked Jesus to forgive his past sin and pride. In my presence, Jack humbly pled for the Holy Spirit to come and live in his soul and guide his future. In time then I was led to officiate his wedding to the right Christian lady the Lord had provided for him. And all along, my occasional Bible studies with his now more spiritually open father enabled Jeff to see that forgiveness was important and possible. The Holy Spirit worked with both to settle their differences and love each other unconditionally, resulting in a happy ending. Even though they still didn't spend a lot of time together, they had peace of mind. They had finally and sincerely <u>pardoned</u> one another's misdeeds.

> " *The first key to stopping the circle of pain...is to accept there is a way to resolve.* "

The first key to stopping the circle of pain in families is to accept that with godly outside help there is a way to resolve the uncomfortable feelings and guilt that comes through years of harm in a dysfunctional family. The second key then is for the parties to accept Jesus as their personal Savior. Usually, however, this healing process must start with that hero. When he is a believer the great Counselor, the Holy Spirit (John 14:26 KJV), will teach him or her what they need to develop softened hearts. Only then will the bitter hero become reconciled with his past, present, and future.

To carry grudges, to continue isolation, to work hard to prove themselves more successful than their parent or to harbor deep resentment—are all sinful ways that rob this affected strong personality from being all that he can or intends to be. Any of these responses are against what God is seeking to build in him. A root of bitterness (Hebrews 12:15) can grow up in the heart like a weedy plant that will eventually protrude through the ground and bloom with all its ugly fullness. But the weed in human life is metaphorically an irrational defensive attitude that causes more trouble for the dysfunctional family. And this poisonous root will even defile or ruin the next (third) generation (Inheritors) of family members. The continued sharp or abrasive posture of the young adult (second-generation or Perpetuator) hero will in turn warp the responses and reactions of their own children. Thus, the grace of God is being missed or held back because that wounded son or daughter never settled their hurt from the first generation-Originator. *We spiritual leaders need to get the Holy Spirit's direction on how and when to approach these wounded young parents with the potent biblical principle of* **forgiveness**. This difficult idea of <u>pardoning</u> the guilty one is very agonizing for the Hero, yet it's very necessary for his peace. And for that matter, the other three types of victimized children must eventually accept this impactful principle of Scripture as well. Let me explain even more.

THE SOLUTION – A NEW IDEA FROM JESUS

As in the parable on how often to forgive in Mathew 18:23-35, Jesus describes how the first debtor to the king, after being mercifully forgiven a great debt, would not be patient with the person who owed him a little money. Likewise, a wounded Perpetuator Christian parent today who continues to carry a grudge against his mean or unloving father or mother is like that first debtor. He or she will become more self-centered, feeling only the harm done to them and wishing to retaliate with the older parent in some cleverly disguised way.

However, the lesson the young parent who was the injured child, needs to learn is that when he was first saved, God forgave him a great debt. Therefore, he cannot continue to be like the first forgiven person in the parable. His unloving parent did him wrong, yes; but since he also was forgiven by the King, he is likewise expected to forgive his own sinful parent in proper response to God's love (Matthew 6:15).

Did you notice, though, the first debtor in Jesus' parable had to suffer serious punishment himself for his lack of forgiveness. He was thrown in prison for thinking then acting improperly. The king had to expose and correct this foolish man for him to see he was ungrateful for the King's heart-felt sympathy and enormous grace. The first debtor was selfish about his own needs, and unwilling and insincere about following the King's great example. His darkened heart would not allow him to see he was unrepentant about his own wrong of refusing to pardon the next friend's debt. The second debtor represents the hero's difficult parent – owing a debt yet expecting mercy. Our Perpetuator-parent is just as blinded or unwilling as the first debtor in the parable.

Theologically speaking to sin on purpose is to do something wrong against God, the King. When we wrong God, we incur a debt that we cannot pay. Repentance is to admit our transgression, to seriously ask HIM to forgive our debt of sin. Connected with those feelings of relief and freedom is the realization that the guilty one doesn't deserve such a pardon. The King's agape love releases the debt. But the first debtor in the parable didn't feel guilty about his own unpaid debt or his insincere thanks for the pardon. He probably felt it was OK to incur such a deficit. In his own worldly mind, like many carnal Christians of today, he felt it was part of the normal ups and downs of life, an unfortunate consequence of working for this boss.

But, in his thinking the money owed to him was a different situation. It was probably as a favor for the friend that the first debtor loaned him money. We can transfer this principle to a modern-day situation. The original Controlling or Conforming parent considers it an act of kindness or duty for their son to pardon the wrong that they committed. And so, on the surface, the Perpetuator child will respond graciously; but in his injured mind he is saying, "I'll overlook this for the sake of public harmony, or so the grandkids are not left out by my real hidden feelings of anger or spite." He will force himself to smile or say kind things, but under his breath he would rather put the parent down or embarrass him or her.

Yet, the bitter young parent of today who wants his dad or mom to pay him back through apology, refuses to see that his anger with them is creating another debt of sin against God. Carrying a grudge or even staying hurt is thinking of oneself, and it is displeasing to the Lord. As God's children, we are to live in a Christ-like manner despite the abuse or neglect we have experienced. When filled with the Holy Spirit, compassion and mercy become the characteristics we can display in response to a difficult person. Paul says to "put away all bitterness, anger, and slander" (Ephesians 4:31-32) and to forgive "just as in Christ God forgave you!"

So then, *when the wounded second-generation dad or mom is open to hearing good advice, the counselor should share several Scriptures on forgiveness. The hope is that in a private time this Perpetuator might ponder on that mercy from God on High. With our praying they may become convicted by the Holy Spirit to forgive the debt of others owed to them. This refers of course, to their parent who abused them. The honest reality that we counselors must share is: Our Heavenly Father forgave our tremendous debt of evil when we asked him to. Likewise, we ought to be willing to forgive a smaller grievance for something wrongly done toward us no matter how big it may seem in our minds. God wants us to think bigger and better.*

REAPING WHAT HE SOWS

Again, the second-generation young adult who is bitter toward his parents is that first debtor in the parable. Despite the heartache experienced, Jesus knows it is best for the suffering one to forgive. But, to demand the Originator, the second debtor, makes things right or apologizes for a past mistake is to selfishly "grab and choke" him; while screaming "Pay back what you owe me!" (Matthew 18:28b). If the young adult remains angry and refuses to <u>pardon</u> his harmful parent, the King will allow him to be tortured until he pays back his debt, until he's willing to forgo or overlook what his parent did wrong. Those living with a "root of bitterness" will likely continue to be miserable while holding a grudge for the rest of that older parent's life, and quite possibly even beyond that! When the Perpetuator Christian refuses to follow Christ's command, he "reaps what he sows." Thus, Jesus' warning comes true, "This is how my Heavenly Father will treat each of you unless you forgive your brother [parent] from your heart" (Matthew 18:35). *The anguish of unsettled feelings will be more "torture" for the one demanding an apology; and I'm saying this to the believer in Christ. The refusal to obey God and repent of sin in the heart will eventually bring serious consequences.*

Therefore, a Christian who knows the Bible will not feel satisfied until he finds a way to <u>forgive</u> his parent for the unfair dysfunctional acts committed against him while growing up. In the Sermon on the Mount Jesus clearly said, "If you forgive other people when they sin against you, your heavenly Father will also forgive you. But if you do not forgive others their sins, your Father will not forgive your sins" (Matthew 6:14-15).

A sidenote here: In this Matthew text Jesus is not talking about salvation of our soul. A single act of disobedience will not cause a Believer to lose his standing with God (salvation). Rather it will bring about a serious fracture in fellowship with the God who has willingly given HIS SON to redeem HIS stubborn child. So, the regular connection and good relationship with God the Father will be taken away but not the promise of heaven. Answers to prayer will be jeopardized. Understanding from the Word will be halted. The joy and excitement of walking with and serving the Lord will be gone until such a bitter believer is willing to follow Paul's admonition in Colossians 3:13, "Bear with each other and forgive one another if any of you has a grievance against someone. Forgive as the Lord forgave you." There will be no sweet spiritual fellowship and peace in his heart. That sounds like spiritual torture to me.

Yes, it's true, the forgiven hero of the dysfunctional family has a lot of his parent's sins of which to let go. If he refuses to let them go, he will suffer much in the miserable years to come because his tormented mind will carry guilt and bitterness for a long time. The Lord may not necessarily chastise this first debtor right away, but HE will certainly hold back HIS blessings. I'm not saying it's easy to overlook the wrong inflicted, but it is still harder to live year after year in sadness or anger because the Perpetuator adult refuses to let go of the misguided chance to blame his Originator parent.

Although anger and plans of retaliation are normal, even expected by friends or urged on by other siblings, they are not what God desires to be dished out to the grandparents of the family. Rather, with supernatural help, according to Ephesians 4:31-32 we can get rid of bitterness and brawling and replace ill feelings with kindness and forgiveness. As noted above, when the Spirit of God lives inside a believing young person (John 14:15-17a, 20, 21), HE provides an overwhelming love and a spirit of overlooking and forbearance. This is real and powerful "pardoning" and is impossible without God's "agape" love (see Luke 18:27).

SUMMARY OF CHARACTERS IN THE PARABLE

Originator	1st generation	2nd debtor in parable
Perpetuator	2nd generation	1st debtor in parable
Inheritor	3rd generation	

EXPLAINING TWO IMPORTANT WORDS

Before I go any further with Jesus' parable on forgiveness, I must make a distinction between the two words "pardon" and "forgive." They are two separate feelings that any emotionally injured son or daughter may experience. In addition, they are two distinct individual actions that often need to take place. Usually, pardoning comes first. Sometimes our Lord expects us to do both when relating to someone who has hurt us. But there may be occasions when it is too hard to do both.

For starters, in the Old Testament we find a powerful verse about our Heavenly Father where the prophet uses both words together. "Who is a God like you, who pardons sin and forgives the transgression of the remnant of his inheritance? You do not stay angry forever but delight to show mercy" (Micah 7:18). Our Lord is ready to pardon and forgive us every time we sincerely ask for it.

But let me explain the difference between the two words. And let me also suggest that as Micah says, usually pardon comes first.

The Bible dictionary defines **pardon**: "to release a person from punishment."[22] Adding to that, Webster says "to absolve from the consequences of a fault or crime, the excusing of an offense." So, I think pardoning is the first requirement when it comes to the full purposeful act of **forgiveness**. Isaiah says that when the wicked turns to God and forsakes his way and the evil man his thoughts, then the Lord will have mercy on him and freely pardon his wrong acts (Isaiah 55:7). God's mercy provides a pardon. When the wicked repent of their ways, HE will release them from their penalty. But that once evil man must then "forsake his thoughts." This will lead him to God's forgiveness through his new desire not to commit that kind of sin any longer.

In a dysfunctional family the victim can pardon any offender when he no longer holds them responsible for the pain and misery they caused. The hurt person decides in mercy to release him from the penalty of his

---

[22] *Liberty Illustrated Bible Dictionary*, Thomas Nelson 1986

actions. There will never be any more thoughts of "blame" such as, "If he would have only done things ... this way". No more replaying the bad scene will be allowed in the sufferer's mind. The inflictor has been "absolved from any consequences"!

> " *The hurt person decides in mercy to release him from the penalty of his actions* "

But next, forgiveness comes when the one deprived of fairness chooses to overlook or take away self-centered thoughts of having the offender still pay for the wrong committed. The victim has released the offender from any punishment. He then goes further by deciding to not feel any frustration or self-pity because the person took wrongful action against him. From here on there is no wish to harm or get back at the person that hurt their feelings, broke good relationships, or even tarnished a positive reputation.

Now in their heart the wounded one may hope that the aggressor will someday wish that he had never participated in the sad situation. Yet, whether the one committing the wrong feels sorry about his deeds or not, by God's grace the hurt person no longer wishes ill toward the used-to-be adversary. In fact, the victim totally turns the problem over to God.

This means leaving the burden of any just retribution to God's perfect vengeance (Romans 12:19) in His way and His time. Now, the wounded one is free from bitterness and can view that individual with grace and godly love. No longer desiring justice himself, the injured person in his mind has given that responsibility totally over to the Righteous Judge. That's where it belongs according to Jesus (I Peter 2:23). This will cause that previously bothered person to feel at peace and good inside because he is obeying the freeing truth of the Lord Jesus.

So, to pardon is to release the offender from any penalty we used to feel was applicable or necessary. Forgiveness is having no more thoughts that the offender must somehow suffer for his actions. Pardon says, "I will no longer hold him accountable or remain angry at him." That is releasing him from the penalty. Forgiveness says "I will no longer hold a grudge nor wish him ill. The offender needs no more suffering".

This serious heart-felt response is also part of the way to process Jesus' command to "love your enemies" (Matthew 5:38-44). If a Christian can release a person who doesn't like him from the need for any personal retribution, the next step is for the love-filled believer to allow the Lord to help him understand there is no longer any room in his heart to hold a grudge or to wish ill of that aggressor. Pardon will also involve releasing the mean person because they don't realize how cruel or self-centered they have been. But the follower of Christ does, and he or she can still allow the Holy Spirit to overwhelm them with supernatural love and choose to forgive the wicked and wrong-thinking one.

Remember that Jesus, while tortured and maligned, looked from the Cross with compassion at HIS enemies. He cried out to God, Father, forgive them, for they do not know what they are doing (Luke 23:34). A brutally battered Christ cites a reason to pardon these beastly soldiers who were just obeying orders. It was habitual and mindless cruelty that they were trained for, and they repeated those actions without conscience or interest in the one they were killing. They had no idea that they were using ferocious force on an innocent, perfect individual. Here I think, the Almighty would pardon their act at Jesus' request but not necessarily forgive the sin in their heart. Jesus was releasing those who hurt him from the just penalty of any physical retribution for their inhuman act of unwarranted torture.

Applying this point to the strong theme of this book, there are many callous or uncaring young adults who are unwilling to pardon their cruel parents even though they were under the wicked spell of inflicting unwarranted torture on their kids. The problem is the unfair flaws became habitual and mindless actions that could have come from the previous generation of dysfunctional parents, the Originators who raised them. *So, it is appropriate to ask newly saved but still bitter moms and dads to consider "pardoning" their own bad parents. It should be their next step. Only the indwelling Holy Spirit can cause this love to develop in a damaged soul - and it is essential the victim arrives there in his heart.*

So, here are my suggestions for resolving conflict between generations in a dysfunctional family. First the younger adult, the Perpetuator, needs to release the older parent from responsibility to set right any damaged feelings or emotional injuries (Pardon). That is just what the king in the parable expected the first debtor to do, to wave the responsibility of the second debtor. And as said earlier, the offensive person doesn't always need to apologize for his wrong. Time can heal. Also, full forgiveness by the wounded Christ-follower can take care of the whole issue with no more bad feelings.

Second, the hurt person cannot decide to make things right in his own way i.e. - no paybacks nor "eye for an eye" mentality. Jesus says that rather than retaliate, the best move is to "turn the other cheek" or walk a second mile with the aggressive person (Matthew 5:38-41). This is to show God's love and to pray that HE will in time miraculously change the deranged heart. I've seen a second-generation mother, convicted by God, pardon and forgive her verbally abusive father. After mentally releasing him, she spent several months actively loving her grouchy dad, surprising him with kind acts, defending him in public, and sending him appropriate gifts. This agape love caused him to have a private conversation with her and to ask forgiveness for his wrong. As chapter 7 indicates "Love is the answer."

By the same token, if some physical injuries have occurred or lawsuits need to be filed, the hurt person must turn to God for answers to legal issues according to another level of circumstances. There are times when the police must be called, or civil services will need to intervene. Official counselors and/or legal professionals may need to be involved in some dangerous family issues. Perhaps restraining orders, supervised visitations, judges' rulings, or even temporary incarcerations might need to be pursued for everyone's safety. Remember the Apostle Peter wrote that God sends those in authority "to punish those who do wrong and to commend those who do right" (I Peter 2:13-14).

So then, conversely, I've also discovered times when forgiveness was necessary, but pardon (release the offender from penalty) could not happen. People can determine to love the cruel ones but not feel good about becoming close again. It is right to forgive, to stop hating or wishing ill, but sometimes it's not best to release a person from the consequences and suffering they brought on themselves. As seen in the previous paragraph, there are times when we can't fully pardon the one who hurt us.

We see this principle clearly demonstrated by God Himself in a story in Numbers 14 in the Old Testament. This is after 10 of the 12 spies refused to go into the Promise Land as God had directed them to. After a public scene and the expression of anger, Moses, the phlegmatic peacemaker, asked God to forgive the sin of the 10 and pardon their rebellion. To this request GOD said, "I have forgiven them as you've asked. Nevertheless, as surely as I live ... not one of those who saw My glory ... but disobeyed me and tested Me 10 times—not one of them will ever see the land" (vv. 20-23). So, God struck them dead on the spot. Plus, He commanded that the other men who followed their evil report should all die in the wilderness over the next 40 years before their grown children would be allowed to enter the Promised Land.

There was no pardon of the penalty. He forgave their selfish thoughts and lack of faith because Moses interceded for them. But He would not pardon their anger at God and refusal to follow His orders. Consequences would be paid. Their offspring felt the loss in the future and certainly understood the reason.

Likewise, today there are consequences to intended acts of transgression, and people often pay for the results for years to come. God is still willing to forgive our selfish thoughts and faulty reasoning. When believers repent and honestly ask for His forgiveness, they always have it. But the bad effect on others may not be taken away or forgotten by them. In time the parties may apologize and ask each other for forgiveness. A second marriage may result, with both couples having peace, and moving on with an improved life. But the kids are often still damaged, even after they are grown. Or, maybe another difficult case could be an irate act of forceful discipline that harms a child physically for most of their future life. In these cases, there could be Forgiveness, yes; but Pardon, perhaps not.

SUFFERING COMPLICATES FORGIVENESS

Now let us return to my points of Family Dysfunction. If our counselee, no matter his personality, does not yet know Christ, we must take a different tact. The application of the parable from Matthew 18 may not resonate in the unsaved mind. They might understand the King's change of judgment when he found out what the first debtor did to the second debtor. But they may never see that they do not have the moral freedom in God's eyes to punish their own absent or demanding parent. They probably feel they have really suffered enough and, to be fair, Mom or Dad should also feel some pain.

Without the Holy Spirit explaining these things, they might just see this parable as an interesting story. But they do not see any hope for change or recognized interest in helping them with their contentious family. *So, for the unsaved we must show a sense of sympathizing with their pain and empathizing with their feelings. As we discuss with them what they are experiencing at home, we should ask questions that show we understand and that we care. We can let them know we feel sorry for them and their difficult experiences.*

We have already shared in this book that God knows what is going on in disappointed hearts. HIS plan for their situation was something different. But Satan has used their parent to hurt them and thwart God's loving purpose for their lives. We believe that our Lord is greater than any devilish plot against them. HIS grace is also stronger than any sin they've experienced from others or have committed themselves. *The person we are working with may even feel that he was unfairly born in a dysfunctional home. Yet here is what Jesus says about helping them to get out of the difficult emotional net they are caught in. "The thief comes only to steal, kill, and destroy; but I have come that they may have life, and have it to the full" (John 10:10).*

The Bible goes on to say that since our trials are common to others in the world, HE has promised to deliver those who know and trust HIM. We should ask the broken one "Are you able to accept that promise now?" God declares HE will not allow HIS Children to be tried beyond what they can bear. He will provide a way out so that any believer can endure it (I Corinthians 10:13, author's paraphrase). *So, the next question needs to be: Can the counselee believe this? Does he or she really want the Lord's help?*

Through years of counseling, I have discovered that nearly all emotionally bruised people can see things only from one side. They are blinded from the whole truth. To be self-consumed is to be self-centered. The victim mindset does not allow a person to see the damage he (even a saved Christian who should know better) is causing others in the family. The one with hurt feelings cares neither to see nor understand how or where others close to him have been affected either by that same harsh family individual or even by his or her own self-interest or self-pity.

Yet, The Psalmist says "It was good for me to be afflicted so that I might learn Your decrees (119:71). The opposite of feeling like a "victim" is learning to trust the Lord for His plan to mature a person in the faith. *Even years of pain in a family of dysfunction, if explained in this way, can eventually help lift the person out of depression and restore adult children to sound reasoning. Continual follow-up on our part can help this individual grow closer to Christ emotionally and spiritually.*

Every person needs to be reminded that we are all sinners. Romans 3:10 says that not one person is good. And verse 23 notes that all people fall short of God's glorious standard. Every human being may have a story of mistreatment or a list of grievances. But, if we are not personally good enough to keep from sinning against our sibling or forebearer, then how will we ever be fair enough to judge one of them for their sins? God alone has the right to punish sin. Only HE can understand the reason and timing for what we say and do.

Yet the unsaved will often try to take that authority or power to themselves. I heard recently of a grown son who tried to disown his mother because of the way she treated him in the past. She was a terrible parent, often leaving him alone while chasing men and drugs. Once she totally failed to keep a special promise to him in high school, and this bitter young man carried his grudge for a long time. He refused to invite his mother to his wedding. The distraught Mom committed suicide shortly after that. Then, feeling terribly guilty, the son became depressed, emotionally damaged, and was unable to keep a job or raise his own family.

We must face the fact that sinful people do sinful things. But godly people can think and do better and will pass their morals on to friends who are watching and wondering. Joseph in the Bible gives us a good example of what to do when family members work against our best interest and basic need. His jealous brothers (as I mentioned in chapter 6) plotted to get rid of their father's favorite son. They were going to kill him but then decided to sell him into slavery. This is familiar material from which even most non-Christians can glean positive points. *I suggest that counselors tell this story from Genesis 39-50 to the unsaved person in their office. It is not a difficult puzzle.* In fact, it is a familiar tale in the secular world, as in the Broadway play put on by many high school drama classes, "Joseph and the Coat of Many Colors."

As you will recall Joseph's story is built on a dysfunctional family. He unfairly went through much trial and danger that revealed God's amazing protection and glorious grace. But this mistreated son had to see that with the Lord's changing of his heart, even as a victim of dysfunction, he could in time gain the power to forgive grizzly brothers and his inattentive, "coddling" father, Jacob. God produced in Joseph a forgiving heart, not just a pardoning mind. This important personal change of view was demonstrated by his tears of love and joy. "You intended to harm me, but God intended it for good to accomplish what is now being done, the saving of many lives. So then, don't be afraid. I will provide for you and your children" (Genesis 50:20-21).

What a wonderful principle for living we have here! No matter the shock, fear, or anger that the Perpetuator parent went through in the past, God wants to get ahold of his or her heart. *He wants to prove through us that the harm the family member sought to do to them, whether purposely or not, can be supernaturally turned into good to accomplish what is now better.*

> " *...the harm ...can be supernaturally turned into good.* "

The passage goes on to say, "And he (Joseph) reassured them and spoke kindly to them" (50:21b) Our Lord desires that dysfunctional families in this age be assured that they can climb out of the pit. The struggle can be conquered. The great hurt can be healed. When the victim is saved or starts to think obediently, Romans 8:28 can bring strength. For those who turn to God, HE promises to work difficult things out for their good, and HIS glory!

HOPE ENABLES FORGIVENESS

To summarize: the believer has the power, against all odds, to do what the Holy Spirit tells him or her to do. The unsaved adult usually does not have that inner strength or special wisdom. *We counselors and pastors need to listen to the victims' stories with great compassion. As we give our advice, we should ask the Lord to help us find ways to lead this person to Christ as Savior.*

They will then be able to find hope that their situation will change. And as they listen to us over time, the Holy Counselor will lead them to the place where they will be willing to release their afflicter from penalty - that's pardon. Then as they are willing to draw closer to Christ, over time their heart will open to full forgiveness.

I once read of a woman growing up in an extremely dysfunctional family. Her parents and three older brothers were all alcoholics. Her mother was mean to her and made her do all the household chores for everyone when she was only 6 years old. She was abused verbally, physically, and sexually while she lived at home.

Phyllis Jennes mentions that she was saved at a church youth group as a teen but was never able to let go of her fear, bitterness, or emotional numbness. But one day after she was married and had children, an evangelist explained that Jesus cancelled her guilt and shame about her past when HE drank the cup of suffering at Gethsemane and calvary (See Matthew 26:42). She then understood that it was for the sin of detesting her mom and the unwillingness to forgive her father and brothers that Jesus died. She was now able to release them from her tortured mind and to no longer hold them responsible for her sadness and guilty feelings. There and then she finally felt relief and cleansing from her holy Master and Savior.[23] Now she had the power to live her life free of the stronghold of victimhood. And she not only pardoned but fully forgave all her cruel family. JESUS is still her PEACE.

The believer must be reminded that until the wounded family member stops holding the enemy accountable (pardon), he will not fully forgive. Until the victim of dysfunction recognizes that he is acting like the first debtor in Jesus' parable, he will be unable to have peace in his heart and move on to a stronger healthier life. In addition, the rest of the broken family will marvel at the strength God supplies. And in time many of them will want to be set free from the pain of dysfunction also.

> *"Until wounded family member stops holding enemy accountable, he will not fully forgive."*

This is the answer to the question I asked in the first paragraph of this chapter. What can stop the hurt from being repeated? When the wounded person can pardon and forgive the one who hurt him, he who had been suffering under dysfunction can finally have peace and confidence. When the sinful parent is released from the crime, and the hurt adult no longer wishes him or her to suffer or experience guilt, all can

---

[23] Phyllis Jennes, "A Witness to God's Grace", quoted in Gloria Gaither, *What My Parents Did Right*, Howard Publishing Co, West Monroe, LA, 2002, 162-64.

have freedom. The painful cycle will not continue, and it will end there. The Perpetuator parent will not repeat the same kind of offence to his children, the Inheritors.

Thus, there is no more reason to remain wounded. There is no more reason to retaliate. There is no more reason to parent their own children with a chip on the shoulder. Now they can raise their kids God's way. Then the "first debtor parent" can love, teach value, protect, and support their adolescents with honesty, sincerity, and clear direction. The curse will not continue! Deuteronomy 5:9 will no longer apply in this family. Victory will be experienced.

Let me close with a personal story about forgiveness. In one of my churches, I was visiting a man who had many valuable collectible items in his house. It was wintertime and I had on a long overcoat. After praying in his living room for his health and blessings on his family, I rose from the couch and accidentally knocked over a rare and expensive vase that was on the coffee table. When it hit the floor, it cracked in three places. I was greatly shocked and apologized profusely, offering to pay to have it fixed or replaced. The wife was upset and said I should just leave, and we would talk about it later.

After a few days, the understanding husband called to say, "It's all right Pastor, the vase was one of many she had, and they weren't that important to her anyway. Alice doesn't want you to have to worry about replacing it!" That was a **pardon**, his wife released me from the penalty of breaking her expensive vase. Then the wife got on the phone. I apologized again. She said, "Pastor, I prayed about this a lot. I don't have any hard feelings toward you. It was clearly an accident. Don't worry about a thing. I'm forgetting about it" That is **full forgiveness**. Hopefully this story puts everything in perspective. *Maybe you can use it in your counseling.*

THE POWER OF FORGIVENESS - SUMMARY OUTLINE

A. Example of the HERO (independent-minded, determined) to study anger and bitterness.
1. The root of bitterness makes it hard to forgive.
2. Carrying a grudge, "Grace of God missed." Hebrews 12:15
3. Two keys to stopping the Circle of Pain.
   a) Believe there is a resolution.
   b) Accept Christ as Savior

B. The Solution – a new idea from Jesus. Matthew 18:23-35
1. Parable about forgiveness – the king and 2 different debtors.
2. Second-generation parent holding on to anger - 1st Debtor.
3. To sin on purpose is to incur a debt you are unable to pay!
4. Repentance is to admit guilt, ask forgiveness, and realize undeserving of pardon.
5. Staying hurt is self-centered and displeasing to God.
6. With God you can feel HIS mercy and strength to put away all bitterness.
7. Bitterness remains for life, as "torture" Matt 18:35. Reap what you sow.

C. Explaining the Difference between Pardon and Forgiveness.
1. Pardon – to release a person from punishment, to excuse an offense. Wounded person turns vengeance totally over to God.
2. Forgiveness - no longer hold a grudge, wish ill on the offender. Jesus said - "Father, forgive them, for they know not what they do." and "Love your enemy".

3. My suggestion for resolving conflict between generations.
   a) Perpetuator (2nd generation parent) must release Originator (older generation) in their mind.
   b) Hurt person cannot decide to fix things, no retaliation. Follow Agape Love!

D. Suffering Complications
   1. God's turnaround plan and additional grace can be strong enough to salvage relationships.
   2. God's promise to not allow us to go through more than we can bear – is much relief.
      a) Common for wounded ones to feel beyond repair. Suffering can be for our good.
      b) As sinners, we cannot be fair in judging other peoples' reasons or motives.
      c) Joseph's story in Genesis – he forgave his jealous and cruel brothers.

E. Hope enables forgiveness.
   1. Phyllis' story of forgiving abusive parents and siblings.
   2. Answer to Question – What can stop the hurt?

Until the wounded family member can stop holding the enemy accountable (pardon), he will not be able to fully forgive. Until the victim of dysfunction recognizes that he is acting like the first debtor in Jesus' parable; he will be unable to have peace in his heart and move on to a stronger healthier life.

Chapter 9

BATTLE IN THE MIND

As we determined in chapter 3, the mind is where life functions. It tells the body how to feel (intellect and emotions), then how and when to make decisions. When the mind or soul is in tune with God, good choices are made. However, when the soul is self-centered, sinful volition often takes control and headstrong or stubborn moves are made.

What we are considering next is how to help those parents who have made poor choices because of their particular bend or personality. What an individual holds in his heart as important determines how he thinks. Our natural mind falls into routines or comfortable ways of living life. The habits we form and the convictions we hold are based on what we hear or learn and then allow to settle in our minds. The ideas that the brain processes can become **strongholds**. Those areas of our mind that we use or refer to most often can be either positive or negative, helpful, or harmful.

" *What an individual holds
in his heart as important determines
how he thinks.* "

The word **stronghold** is an interesting one. To have a "strong" "hold" is to grab something tightly, of course; with no intention of letting go. But when the two words are put together, the emphasis is on a place or situation that protects or stabilizes a person. David hid among the large rocks or caves in the wilderness when King Saul was chasing him to end his life. He called it a stronghold. Also, in the Old Testament a "stronghold" was a location where people could place themselves above any danger and stay fortified with weapons should any enemy try to capture or defeat them. It was a safe, comfortable place where one could remain for a long time, being unmovable until the occupant himself chose to leave. Metaphorically, a stronghold can be a comfortable thought that remains in the mind and becomes a habitual desire. In such a case, that idea would be unmovable until a contrary thought was allowed to move in and take its place.

The Apostle Paul tells Christians that they should "destroy strongholds" that are placed in their minds by evil forces (2 Corinthians 10:4). So, what he's talking about is demolishing or annihilating – not just moving out – thoughts or ideas that would cause believers to doubt God's intensions and power. Our subject in this book is dysfunctional families, but in this chapter I want to focus on flawed parents who are Christians. I want to apply this challenge to overcoming the bad habits or ungodly attitudes that have taken over the lifestyles of weaker believers who are not following the wisdom and ways of Jesus.

Now I have discovered that there are 3 levels of strongholds that Christians must make serious decisions about. Level one is the least harmful, but the easiest to fall into. The second level has to do with the kinds of societal changes that our American society is going through right now. And the third level that believers face is the most dangerous and the hardest to defeat. Let me show you what I mean.

<u>A - Minor selfish life patterns</u> – 1st Level Strongholds are personal habits we develop.

Negative <u>strongholds</u> that Christian parents allow to sneak into their lifestyles may include:

- insisting that they are right all the time.
- doubting that God can or will use them to do special things.
- not focusing on what their mates are trying to tell them about their personal feelings.
- not taking time to sit down with teen children to lovingly discuss what's important to them in their busy lives.
- being habitually late for gatherings or family plans, and thinking it is not a problem.

We tell ourselves that these unhealthy habits do not really matter. Yet Scripture says we are to think of the wellbeing of others ahead of ourselves (Philippians 2:4). However, to insist on our way and not pay attention to what others in the family ask or need of us is to disobey God's will. If we think we're more important than our spouses, our children, or our work partners, we are living by worldly standards. We are sinning against them without realizing it or without caring what God says. All of us are guilty to some extent and need Christ's help to stop loving ourselves too much. We must let God's love work through us. As Paul says in 1 Corinthians 13, we can do a lot of good things, even religious things, but if we do not have agape love, "we are nothing" (v. 2) and like an inharmonious gong (v. 1). As such, God cannot effectively use us.

When believing adults find themselves tending toward selfishness or are told that their words or actions are not very encouraging to those around them, they should humbly go to the Lord for help. When we lack insight or proper motivation, the Bible says we are to ask God for direction. "If any of you lacks wisdom, he should ask God, who gives generously to all without finding fault, and it will be given him" (James 1:5). Here we are told that God wants to be asked and to give answers that will sustain us. HE may respond to our prayers by putting new thoughts in our minds or through an unexpected encounter with another person who has keen advice that really fits our situation.

Christian parents have a clear advantage to help them when faced with confusion, uncertainty, or even temptations. It is the Holy Spirit living inside the minds of mature moms and dads that make the difference. So, they have the capability to refute all the lies and resist all the wrong desires or habits that Satan often causes them to focus on. James 1:14-15 says it is up to the individual Christian to decide whether he will be dragged away or enticed by pursuing his own evil thoughts. The Spirit-led dad or mom can take the better road by opting to "Resist the devil, and he will flee from you" (James 4:7).

Herein lies the tough choice – will the believer follow God, or will he/she listen to the wrong thoughts Satan is daily trying to entice them with? *The experienced Bible-based counselor can bless the Christian dysfunctional parent by clearing up confusion. The spiritually wandering adult who is making wrong decisions for their children can be helped by finding the reason for their choices. You can also suggest to them how to discover God's will in handling current options.*

Zeroing in again on our four "flawed parents," consider a few questions about choices:

- Should a cruel, choleric father continue to be a bully, inflating his ego to the detriment of his kids?
- Should the melancholy mom insist that the rest of the family do her wishes by teaching her children to do life the way she wants, so she can feel better about herself?
- How about the chaotic dad excusing his lack of discipline or time at home by insisting that the rest of the clan have enough things to keep them from being bored?
- And the happy-go-lucky, sanguine mom selfishly spoiling her kids, later frantically complains to her teenage daughter, "Why won't you tell me what you're thinking?"

These damaging examples all point to wrong choices. Individual personality or temperament has much to do with this. Yet, I believe there is a deep longing for significance in life that plays the major part in parents managing poorly. This is why I spent more detailed time on shame and poor self-image in chapters 4 and 6. Furthermore, the way they learned to respond to troubles at home frequently overrides what God says is the moral or honest way of doing things.

> " *I believe there is a deep longing for significance.. that plays a major part in parents managing poorly.* "

Counselors should remind the flawed Christian parents that true significance in life comes from their growing relationship with the reconciling Lord and their willing obedience to His Word. Parents can trust Christ to guide them in all their decisions. They can be sure that the All-knowing One wants to give His wisdom and peace when the believer is faced with the many family choices in life. "Show me your ways O Lord, teach me your paths. Guide me in your truth and teach me, for you are God my Savior, and my hope is in you all day long" (Psalm 25:4-5).

Yes, even adult Christians who may be weak in their faith can find balance. They should try to function somewhere between providing what their spouse and children need and by pursuing legitimate desires of their own. They must have God's wisdom to achieve an even keel to be able to lead toward that balance. But when a controlling or disorganized dad chooses himself first, the whole family suffers because the Lord was not consulted. Likewise, when a partial mom insists that only her kids' wants are primary, the husband-wife relationship will usually suffer. These are illustrations of unspiritual human wisdom rather than God's pure, peace-loving guidance. (James 3:16-17) *We must help them work toward balance.*

B - Unbiblical, immoral ideas – 2nd Level Strongholds are worldly concepts pushed on the mind.

Now there are other, more serious examples of satanic strongholds that need to be challenged quickly and demolished in the minds of the children and teens especially from households of nominal or carnal Christians. Through magazines, movies, television, and the Internet, secular society has bombarded the eyes and brains in America with immoral and ungodly ideas. Furthermore, university campuses and even public high schools have permitted foolish ideas to be taught and even demonstrated. In addition, the judicial system has bought into this corrosive way of thinking, and ACLU lawyers have won cases to allow freedom of speech to include what the Apostle Paul calls "shameful lusts" and "unnatural relations," proclaimed by wicked and "depraved minds." (See Romans 1:26-28). So, many moral-thinking and church-going parents are allowing their Christian young people to fill their minds with such evil philosophies that can become **strongholds**. They are likely to hear such false claims as:

- Any woman has a right to choose an abortion by herself.
- Young people should be allowed to change their sex and gender if they want to.
- I can put into my body whatever substance or beverage I feel like.
- A little pornography is OK for a young man. It's part of life.
- It's OK to protest; it's the American way, even if it turns violent.
- Only certain parts of the Bible are from God, and we must figure out which are for us.

What others teach or recommend can lead innocent people to make bad choices. Believing adults should be on guard because engrained strongholds can form quickly. Although the Holy Spirit lives inside their souls, Christians of a young age must still go through the personal decision-making process to choose right or wrong. Influenced by various environments and because they still have the sinful nature, growing kids often choose selfishly or in a way that displeases their Lord. They may know better but can't always do what's right. Peer pressure and social media are very strong persuaders! As Paul himself testified, "For I know that good itself does not dwell in me, that is, in my sinful nature. For I have the desire to do what is good, but I cannot carry it out" (Romans 7:18).

The six examples just listed as false claims are really what the Scripture calls "pretensions". We will deal more specifically with this effective word later in this chapter. But let me next go to the third level of strongholds. Now we are going further than just persistent relational issues in the family, or false teaching taught by people we would otherwise trust. Now Satan has upped his game - and is reaching beyond hurt feelings and confused minds. His next more costly target is stealing the souls of both the Perpetuator Parents and Inheritor teens. Remember Jesus said in John 10:10, the devil comes to "steal, kill, and destroy". I believe the "stealing" part is something he is able to do with the Children of God now!

C - Demonic, life-altering traps – 3rd Level Strongholds are evil control of the soul

I have mentioned Satan and his ghastly work already in this book. Chapter 3 talked about the sneaky role he plays in temptation for both believers and unbelievers. In Chapter 5 we discussed how the devil has been attacking our nation through his clever work of destroying public morality, caring responsibility, and family stability. Lucifer has another level of hidden spiritual warfare that is being used potently and repeatedly in our sleepy communities. Ever since the hippies in the late 1960s, the drug culture and the use of opioid pills has specifically taken the heart and motivation out of teens and young adults. It is true that the devil has used disease and starvation to kill large groups of people since the beginning of time. However, narcotic meds and synthetic pills have never been so powerful or in so great astronomical quantity in history as they are now. Just today as I write, the news reports that enough fentanyl is illegally smuggled into the USA through the Southern border to kill 300 people a day.

In the Book of Revelation John saw four horsemen riding as the seal judgments at the beginning of the Great Tribulation period. The fourth rider was on a pale horse which represented death and was given the power to kill a quarter of the population of the earth. The means of annihilating that number of humans all at once is by sword, famine, pestilences, and wild beasts (6:8). "Pestilence" refers not only to a pandemic of disease, but other types of health issues as well, such as drug abuse.

In Revelation 9 we see the blowing of the Trumpets that unleash a series of more plagues upon the whole earth, probably starting in the middle of the Tribulation. The Greek word in verse 21 is *pharmakeia* from which we get pharmacy. It is translated variously as "magic arts" NIV, "sorceries" (KJV and NAS), and "witchcraft" (NLT & CEV). The rest of mankind that were spared from the first plagues are described as being involved in demonology, sexual immorality, and murderous activity. It sounds like the earth will then be filled with great wickedness where every inclination of the thoughts of the human heart was evil all the time, as it was right before God destroyed it with the Great Flood (Genesis 6:5). In the future end of times, I believe civilization will also be heavily influenced with the power of rampant narcotics producing anarchy and death.

Dopamine molecules (hormones produced in the brain that transmit chemical messages) are greatly agitated by drugs and alcohol. The section of the brain where the cravings and the sensation for emotional joy resides is in the limbic system. Chemicals in illicit drugs greatly increase the release of this dopamine. The strong tendency to need these chemicals builds a "reward pathway" of cells that produces powerful cravings that cannot be easily altered. Thus, addiction comes because the need for more dopamine production takes over the action of the mind of the drug user. So, there is constant demand for more of the life-controlling substance of which the brain is being deprived. This is chemical addiction.[24]

Pastor and Evangelist Tony Evans defines addiction well in his small paperback book *Thirty Days to Overcoming Addictive Behavior*. In his opening chapter he explains addictions as, "go-to coping mechanisms for life's pain, disappointments, or boredom which bring actions or activities that influence a person more than they can influence it."[25] He believes that dependence on alcohol, drugs, gambling, too much work or shopping, all can become strongholds in the mind of a trapped individual. He defines a stronghold as a negative, destructive pattern of

---

[24] Dr. David Irvine, *Introduction to Chemical Dependency*, Addiction Seminar University of Pittsburgh, Johnstown, PA Summer 2019
[25] Dr. Tony Evans, *Thirty Days to Overcoming Addictive Behavior*, Harvest House Publishers, Eugene, OR, 2017, 7.

thinking developed in our minds through repetition, traumatic experiences, or shocking circumstances.

When an addiction or mental stronghold controls a person, his or her mind is more susceptible to Satan's influence. The person is off guard mentally and spiritually by a dopamine influx. The conscience is weakened, the ability to rationalize toward common sense is hindered, and self-control quickly goes out the window. Therefore, the captured mind may hallucinate, dream of scary things, experience delusional thinking, even hear voices. I believe these are perilous signs of demonic activity taking over through the dangerous controlled substance.

The Apostle Paul warns in Ephesians 6 that life's real battles are waged in the mind with rulers and authorities of the darkness of this world or spiritual wickedness in high places (v. 12). The Devil wants to get a stronghold in all people including Christians. And this stronger mental fortress is like a third level of weakened, irrational thought that poisons people for long periods of time. So, a substance abuse often leads to uncontrollable demonic power. Again, we are talking about a real and dangerous stronghold. Many of the flawed parents who have continued in their sin and the weak tendency to yield to certain temptations (chapter 3) are no doubt severely captured by an ultra-strong life trap, illicit drugs.

In Mark 9:29 Jesus points out the seriousness of evil spirit power in the encounter with a demonic spirit that the inexperienced disciples tried unsuccessfully to cast out of a teenage boy: "This kind can come out only by prayer and fasting." Yet Christ was more than capable of casting out the demonic spirit. Spiritual leaders of today, when filled with His Spirit and committed to righteousness over wickedness, can likewise cast out demons. (See Acts 16:18)

Now, I do not believe the true Christian can be possessed by the devil. The Holy Spirit will not leave room in a Child of God's soul for an evil spirit to dwell there. But in a Christian's backsliding and purposeful life of sin, he or she can be greatly oppressed and confused. When observing such a weak anemic believer, it is difficult to determine whether such a disobedient, carnal person truly belongs to the Lord. Yet, if we have information that confirms such a person as a believer, we should seek to help him to be delivered from Lucifer's oppressive clutches.

Therefore, *we counselors may encounter a family issue where we find ourselves directly dealing with the devil. If so, we must prayerfully claim the Blood of Christ and sincerely plead with God to remove the mysterious demon from the unsaved soul, who is causing much of the family chaos. I recommend other mature and confident believers to be with you as you attempt this kind of biblical move. When we are earnestly close to Christ, we have supernatural power as we humbly but bravely and confidently call on HIM to have great victory over the evil spirit and to cast it out. Or if a saved person – to remove the demon from oppressing his/her mind.*

Let us go back now to 2 Corinthians 10 and study closely what it says about strongholds. In verses 4 & 5 Paul writes:

"The weapons we fight with... have divine power to demolish <u>strongholds</u>. We demolish arguments and every pretension that sets itself up against the knowledge of God, and we take captive every thought to make it obedient to Christ."

In this passage we find three truths we need to trust and follow.

- We must fight wrong ideas in our minds, which are strong-holds, with <u>divine power</u>, not with worldly weapons, v. 4. (Spiritual weapons are defined in Ephesians 6 and here at the end of this chapter.)
- Every <u>pretension</u> versus the knowledge of God can be <u>demol-ished</u>, v. 5a. (the basis for victory over the enemy)
- It is possible to <u>take captive</u> all our thoughts and turn them to ways that obey Christ, v.5b. (*This is what we need to study more and ask God for His insight for us to share clearly and carefully with whatever generation we are counseling. You can check my five steps below*).

Let us look at two of these important principles that are particularly relevant to dealing with unbiblical and immoral ideas. We will discuss them hermeneutically (using principles of interpreting and explaining verses) and apply them to dysfunctional parents.

1. Fight our spiritual enemy with <u>divine power</u>

   Divine power is used in the New Testament two other times. Peter says it is a supernatural change of heart and spirit that causes us to not only think like Christ, but also to be able to live like HIM as we learn more and more about HIS message and calling for us (2 Peter 1:3). Then in Romans chapter 1 Paul shows us that a portion of the power God used to create the world (v. 20), and then raise Jesus from the dead (v. 4), is available to his true followers in ways we could not imagine. As we submit to HIM and use HIS gifts in helping people and spreading the gospel (v. 16); we will recognize HIM taking over our thoughts and words. *That is "divine," and is very important for us counselors to show.*

The seriously believing parents can receive astounding power to change their situation and raise their children effectively. Because the battle is one for minds and souls, a person must realize anew that the responsibility of dad and mom is to teach and train, explaining biblical principles as well as they can. Then comes the necessity to teach their growing kids by example how these precepts can be lived out. Also necessary is correction in a loving way and discussion about why and how they should all be pleasing God together as a family. Perhaps churches also should spend some time showing or modeling principles and methods of the verse "Fathers, do not exasperate your children; instead bring them up in the training and instruction of the Lord" (Ephesians 6:4). Divine Holy Spirit power is what's needed in every home to keep it from becoming dysfunctional.

2. Demolish <u>pretensions</u> that war against GOD

Next, principle #2 - what needs to be demolished with divine power? In Greek *hupsoma*, means a high thing or exalting idea. In other words, it is a high and lofty thought, something that makes a person feel proud of their knowledge and status. It may lead someone to doubt God or even to resist HIS will even though he or she has been taught previously that a certain deed or opinion displeases the Lord.

Examples of lofty thoughts might include:

• Science has adopted the theory of evolution, so we don't need God and creation to know where we've come from.

- College-age believers are taught to accept and promote false and exaggerated information about Global Warming, even though contrary facts are convincing also.

- Christian teachers in public high school may buy into the critical race theory that Caucasian people are born prejudiced against African Americans. Thus, they can say it's important to emphasize to their students the need to repent of that racial pride so they can make it up to minority races.

This kind of thinking is leading young people away from the biblical and moral principles they've been taught. Many Millennial parents today are poor examples of caring for their small children and teaching them to love their neighbors and classmates because the grownups have been persuaded otherwise by false teaching professors in our universities. Countless Christian teens are influenced by liberal public-school teachers to discredit the Bible and to believe that no one has the right to tell them what is right or wrong. These are **pretensions**, and they purposefully put doubt in young minds concerning morals, sexuality, lack of purpose, and life-controlling substances. Since this has been happening for decades in our colleges, many of the Busters and Millennials raised in Christian homes have turned away from the Truth and are believing that abortion and sex-change are rights to which they are entitled as well. This drastic switch of convictions has created a new culture of disrespect in homes, great generation divisions, irreparable family arguments, serious political biases, and even many difficult divorces. All these wrong actions and improper reactions create dysfunction before responsible adults realize it is happening. Many times, it is too late to patch up without outside counsel to apply principles of agape love and spiritual forgiveness. (See again chapters 7 & 8.)

"*This drastic switch of convictions has created a new culture of disrespect.*"

These earthly lies are clearly false arguments that oppose the teachings of Christ. Since they are against what Scripture says about godliness, even the casual Christian parent should try hard to not allow his or her child to follow these false pretensions. Nor should he or she talk favorably about, approve of, or joke about them. (See Ephesians 5:3-4). If Satan is permitted to persuade the young adults in the family (the Inheritors) to think this way of loose morals, dad and mom are opening their entire family to the destruction that evil humans and demonic fiends want so much. (See Romans 1:28, 32) These changed, depraved minds, will continue to spread perverted lies to their siblings, neighbors, old classmates, and others.

A mature, biblically prone adult outside the immediate family must prayerfully look for opportunities to graciously counter these pretensions and to lovingly point out to the rebellious one that God will never forget them; and that the Holy Spirit will continue to work at drawing them back. *Counselors can remind the worried adults, as well as the proud younger person, that serious, faith-filled, and passionate prayer to God can bring about situations over time that change the wayward mind. Proverbs 15:29, Isaiah 55:6-7, Matthew 21:22, 1 John 5:14-15 are verses we can use with people about urgent prayer for family repair.*

So then, how else do we fight against this onslaught from the dark world? Well, let's remember that these wrong ideas are **strongholds** that are causing the brains of our children and young adults to be processed in ungodly, even unnatural ways to "determine how he thinks" and to build in her "convictions (opinions) that are contrary to the knowledge of God." To discuss these opposing views carefully and lovingly at appropriate times in the home is a starting point in **demolishing** them. For in this kind of scenario, we even have dysfunction coming first from the children, not a flawed parent.

In his pamphlet, *Speaking the Truth in Love* Steven Huff credits his dad and mom for keeping him and his brother aware of important reasonings and decisions in life. Many times, Dad would keep the teens talking way past midnight about a certain issue and viewpoint until they would arrive at a good, godly conclusion. His father's phrase for this kind of sacrificial care for impressionable youth was, "you have to keep the wound open to clean it out!" The boys learned that their parents loved them enough to let them express their feelings, as well as accept the influence of good or bad outsiders. The wise adults would share their biblical views on how a Christian could handle a certain thing with the Holy Spirit's help. The reaction then at school or work was their choice to make. In this author's words, "My parents earned respect from us; they didn't demand it!"[26]

Whether we are talking about young adults who want to hang onto their new "convictions" or are working with teens/adolescents at home who are just feeling their way through discovering "real truth" – they are actually pretensions! It is essential then, that we remember what the spiritual weapons are and how to encourage victims of false teaching, neglect, or abuse to use them. Ephesians 6:17-18 tells us there are two offensive weapons Christians can employ. The sword of the

---

[26] Stephen Huff, "Speak the Truth in Love" quoted in Gloria Gaither, *What My Parents Did Right*, Howard Publishing Co., West Monroe, LA, 2022, 145-146.

spirit (the Bible) and prayer in the Spirit are the true demolishers of wrong strongholds.

The *spiritual sword* is the Scriptures, of course. We can graciously share them with the confused one, or even his bad influencer. At the right time God may provide specific verses that will convince them that a loving God has a better way for each of them to live.

Prayer is the older family members pleading with the Lord to change the hearts of those who are taking on a different view of life and acting out in self-defense or pride. Perhaps the newly educated ones are finally feeling important or accepted with their strange new ideas since they were not valued nor given the opportunity to be themselves while at home. Or maybe they reason that they are ready to break the mold and discover new concepts and principles without following the old-fashioned opinions forced on them when they were still in the nest.

Since these new wild views of the world and society dispute what the Bible says, h*ere is where the counselor or pastor comes in. He or she can share personal illustrations of truth, good short videos clarifying the tenants of the faith, or brief booklets defending often-used verses of Scripture. This, coupled with prayer to God to open eyes and wash away any spiritual blindness caused by Satan (see 2 Corinthians 4:4) may be the best or only means of restoring them.*

If we are working with children or young teens, we must find clever and spirit-led ways to introduce them to the Word of God also. Interesting personal examples, specific Bible stories, and applicable verses can be presented on their level of understanding. If we are working with a young adult who is a victim of dysfunction, we may be able to explain the need to become familiar with the living principles of Scripture. Understanding what the Heavenly Father has for them or who they really are in Christ

- forgiven, cleansed, chosen, filled, and empowered - can help them feel loved and significant. They've probably never been told of or experienced this inner strength before. Second Timothy 3:16-17 and the Beatitudes of Matthew 5:3-12 can be studied and explained for help to show them that God is on their side to bring them back to HIM no matter how low they feel or what wrong they have done.

Now these spiritual weapons can also be applied to the second-generation children of dysfunction who are now newer parents. I am referring to the millions of Christians in our country who are struggling with their personal hurt from the past. They are sitting in our pews or chairs, and saying "Amen" to our sermons, yet at the same time, they are battling in their minds against the wrong habits and dealings under which they were raised. These precious Perpetuators want with all their heart to do better. They need help to deal with their negative, worldly strongholds. They earnestly desire to be set free from any ungodly pretensions that are still lurking in their minds. That is why they are there on Sunday mornings.

However, hidden hatred for a cruel dad might be their stronghold. Not wanting to take the grandchildren to visit a controlling mom is a stronghold. Lavishing the children with many toys and tools like dad did when money was tight, is probably a bad habit. And plain indifference about proper morals or necessary discipline as their inactive mom had, is a mindset that needs demolishing.

So, after looking at the three levels of strongholds, their negative impact on dysfunctional parents, and the spiritual power that can absolutely demolish them, *we must ask God to give us wisdom and insight to truly guide our clients through victory.* It is important to recognize again that from 2 Corinthians 10:4-5 God gives us <u>divine power</u> to use with the spiritual weapons to counter arguments and <u>pretensions</u> against the knowledge of God. Such strongholds can be captured by Christ as HE leads us to demolish them.

3.   <u>Take captive</u> wrong ideas and allow the Word of God to direct us. In Principle 3, let's look at how trapped Christian people can take captive their wrong thoughts and turn them into obedient ideas and plans that will set them on the straight path that God intended for them.

The Apostle Peter refers to the supernatural ability to "escape the corruption of this world" and to trust GOD's "great and precious promises" (2 Peter 1:4). When anyone trapped and damaged by family dysfunction in any of the three stronghold levels is ready and willing to turn their lives and future over to the living Lord, they will be able to truly "demolish strongholds" (2 Corinthians 10: 4b). *We can advise counselees with wise decisions in capturing any wrong thoughts via the following five steps:*

   a   **Follow after God** with a sincere, humble, willing heart attitude. (See Psalm 119:9-16.) Humility means they must agree that they need the Loving God's help. They cannot resolve their unjust issues or corrupt thoughts alone. Meditating on God's word brings peace and then delight to the soul. Encouragement from another believer helps the snared one to keep going with renewing and freeing attitudes.

Satan will try to block the discouraged person from reading the Bible. The inability to correctly understand what he's reading is a noted example of how demons work. When determined, however, the saved person will be able to rebuke the work of the oppressing demon in their mind. When pleading the blood of Jesus to cover them, our counselee will be able to focus better on wise and heavenly aims (Revelation. 12:11). Then, when ready to ponder on the words of Scripture and apply its directives to their own personal situations, the believer will be able to resist the enemy. James 4:6b-8a tells us that when we humble ourselves before the Lord, not only will Satan flee, but God will draw close.

b **Acknowledge** that the newer ideas and plans they are hearing or living by are wrong, destructive, and enslaving. Again, they are usually ungodly pretensions. Many secular teachers have lost a tenderness toward righteousness. Turning to Christ's teaching will make more sense and provide courage to change the weary one's notions and actions. They must allow the Holy Spirit to work on and in their soul. (See Ephesians 4:17-24). The darkness of sin and idolatry causes loss of sensitivity, hearts to harden, and stronghold habits to form. Yet the light of Jesus' true principles brings new self-awareness, new attitudes, and new righteousness.

c **Pray** to the loving and holy God with **repentance** on their minds and sorrow in their hearts (Acts 3:19). This is asking for forgiveness and admitting they have sinned, then moving pride aside and allowing God to do the demolition work. "Godly sorrow" produces great desire to do right, sheer love for justice to be done, and more concern for others' well-being (2 Corinthians 7:9-11). Repentance calls for divine power to take over!

"*Repentance calls for divine power to take over.*"

d   **Determine** with the Holy Spirit's help and a sincere heart of change to work continually on bringing their daily thoughts into captivity to the obedience of Christ. This means surrendering their wishes and dreams to the Lord. It means being reminded again of who they are in Christ, HIS representatives who are bought, cleansed, forgiven, changed, and empowered. And so, HE will definitely live through them (Galatians 2:20). In other words, they can earnestly ask "WWJD, what would Jesus do?" and proceed to trust the Lord and watch Him direct their paths (Proverbs. 3:5-6).

e   **Commit to a new godly obedience of thought** (or method of change) to:

1)   Reading and studying God's Word, willingly, regularly, and excitedly.

2)   Working with a mentor or strong believer to change habits (more than basic discipleship).

3)   Crying out to the Lord for courage to submit to Him daily and to long for release from Satan's tactics.

4)   Worshiping the Lord continually and fellowshipping with other Christians in a church and in other venues.

As these revived or even renewed believers seek to overcome their embarrassment of the past and uncertainty of the future and as they ponder the reality of Jesus' great love for them, they will have the means to overcome. The battle for their mind will be won by God as they begin to understand that they can truly trust HIM. As King Jehoshaphat called out in 2 Chronicles 20:6c, "Power and might are in your hand, and no one can withstand you." The people of Judah were saved from a vast enemy army as they marched in faith and sang praises to HIM!

As today's believers are at first struck by fear or doubt in the traps of life, they will find victory by moving forward in trusting Christ. They will rejoice in His promises and peace. Before long they will desire the supernatural power to forgive those who have abused or ravaged them in their home (chapter 8). Those looking to conquer bitterness, anger, sadness, or fear will remember the "full armor of God" that HE has provided and will gather the strength to use them and to stand firm. (Ephesians 6:13-17):

- **Belt of Truth** is stability around the waist because the truth keeps us balanced.
- **Breastplate of Righteousness** on the chest for strength as doing right keeps us upright.
- Feet fitted for balance by the **Gospel of Peace**, the salvation story gives reason to go to others.
- **Shield of Faith** moveable and free to repel the devil's fiery arrows; faith blocks lies.
- **Helmet of Salvation** to keep us thinking clearly and our minds ready to fight.

This armor will show the battered mind how to find real emotional comfort and the ability to make sure it doesn't repeat the psychotic practices they were scarred with for years. God is for us and allows us to conquer in His love. In Romans 8:27, 28, 32, 34, & 37 we find the Trinity promises to provide all we need to be strong followers of Christ. Jesus is now in Heaven praying for us Christians, especially when we are accused or feel weak from mysterious mental or spiritual nets.

These Romans 8 verses convince us of significant Truth we need to claim as our own. Father God is the One "who searches our hearts"; therefore, HE knows (v-27) our personal issues and needs very well. The Holy Spirit then can show us God's will in each situation because HE promises in the Word to work on our behalf, as we have been (v-28) chosen and called before our birth to serve HIM. Since the Father gave HIS SON to die for us (v-32), the Gospel message proves our Lord will gift us with timely answers because HE greatly loves HIS own! And that is YOU! So, Jesus prays for you to be lifted up and empowered (v-34) – when you ask for HIS guidance! Then verse 37 reminds us that with Christ close to us we can "conquer" any past mistake, any current temptation, and any future shame we may feel because of selfish, neglectful, or misguided parents.

Oh Counselor, pray earnestly that some in the family you are working with will believe these important truths and live for them! Help them "put on the armor" in their minds and hearts!

BATTLE IN THE MIND - SUMMARY OUTLINE

A. Explanation of strongholds -
   Three levels to consider:
   1. Minor selfish life patterns
   2. Unbiblical immoral ideas
   3. Demonic life altering traps

B. Weapons against strongholds and capturing thoughts for Christ
   Three principles to pursue:
   1. Fight our spiritual enemy with "divine power".
      Parents should teach and demonstrate Biblical principles.
   2. Demolish pretentions that war against God.
      a) Starting point is discussing at home
      b) Two offensive weapons are Word of God and Prayer.
   3. Take captive wrong ideas.
      a) Follow after God.
         Stay humble, resist Satan, meditate on Scripture
      b) Acknowledge the Wrong.
         Loss of sensitivity versus new sense of awareness
      c) Pray with Repentance.
         Godly sorrow, love for justice, concern for others
      d) Determine a Method of Change.
         Holy Spirit filling, biblical thoughts, "crucified with Christ"
      e) Commit to a New Daily Plan.
         Study the Bible, work with a mentor, submit to Lord regularly, worship God, and fellowship with Christians.

Put on the "Armor of God" Ephesians 6:11

*Belt of Truth *Breastplate of Righteousness *Gospel of Peace * Shield of Faith

*Helmet of Salvation

Romans chapter 8 has verses that convince us we have been chosen. God promises to use and protect us for HIS glory as we seek to stay close to HIM!

UNIT IV

VICTORY FOR THE DYSFUNCTIONAL FAMILY

Chapter 10 – Traits of a Healthy Home

Chapter 11 – Positive Lessons in Suffering

Chapter 12 – United Effort

Unit IV

VICTORY FOR THE DYSFUNCTIONAL FAMILY

The house where a person grows up has a tremendous impact on what he or she becomes! Within the walls and under the roofs of the dwellings where kids spend their young years of greatest influence are noises, touches, and sights that can be very encouraging or very damaging to the mind of a child.

Dads and Moms must be diligent at what they present and what they allow as the newer generation forms their opinions, develops their doubts, creates their courage, and raises their hopes for the destined future.

In this Unit I start with a pattern for a strong, healthy home. I call it "A Functional Family". We see seven characteristics that wise parents seek to establish in their house. Examples are honesty, morality, and building in children's hearts a sense of worth and value.

Next, I talk candidly about suffering. Children growing up in broken homes often wonder why they must suffer at the hands of cruel parents, when their peers or relatives their age do not seem to experience that. So, we will find reasons why bad things happen; and ways to overcome the unfortunate issues and lasting impressions these victims must deal with.

The last chapter addresses the need to work on encouraging the local families enduring the pain of disharmony and depression. This help comes through the united efforts of ministry from the whole church, additional professional workers in the community, or other effective programs already established to win many people to wholeness.

Chapter 10

TRAITS OF A HEALTHY HOME

There are tremendous long-lasting results in a home where both parents are aware that their children are extraordinary gifts from God. They often think of the day each baby was born—all the joy and admiration that the infant brings to relatives and friends. Then there is the excitement of parents, perhaps older siblings as well, coming home from the hospital to a special room prepared with love and care for the new member of the household. All the pictures and videos are kept to review the joy God brought into their lives with this child.

Everyone is determined to love this new family member with all they have, holding or lifting up the baby every chance they get. These encouraging parents understand deep within that sacrificing for this precious child is to be a major priority in their lives. And they quickly discover that they must privately ask to receive supernatural assistance to nurture their offspring in the best way. They know they cannot care for the child well enough on their own.

Second-generation (or Perpetuator) parents from a dysfunctional house, however, cannot fathom or develop such a mindset without help from above and/or outside their family. The day the baby came home has long been forgotten. And the enthusiasm and wonderful anticipation has not turned out in quite the way they thought it would. Many issues and pressures of poor relationships work together to make the arrival of a new family member less than memorable.

First, they were influenced wrongly by the previous generation they came from—babies are nice, but not as important as some think. I tried to explain this unfortunate attitude in the first two chapters of this book. Or second, they have developed negative patterns of living such as being controlled by the satanic temptations and/or strongholds they've allowed to grow in their troubling lifestyle through the years (see again chapters 3 and 9). To think of the children first is foreign to them, and to seek help to do things better is either an attack on their pride or too hard to program in their selfish minds. Even backslidden Christians can fall into such a negative darkened trap.

IMPORTANT WORK FOR A FUNCTIONAL FAMILY

But the good news is that many adults in our nation do work hard at raising their kids to be good, positive examples. They fight the busyness, being away in the evenings, or bringing their work home. They insist on a schedule and design their week to give equal time and attention to each child. Arrangements are made to sit down and discuss what is going on at school with their studies, teachers, friends, and attitudes. This is part of the "functional family;" and we *need to show the example that is possible to the folks we have felt led to come alongside because of family brokenness. Hope needs to be pictured in the counselor's mind first, and then in theirs.*

Great care is given by these mature parents to not miss their children's functions, musical or athletic events, even church plays and to make sure that vacation time is well planned and spent with the whole family. Goals are privately established together by dad and mom to love each individual child with equal effort. Things are done deliberately at home and in public to point out that every child is valuable and important to the whole group. Steps are taken to eliminate offending others as much as possible. Fairness and kindness are explained regularly to each sibling. Rules and patterns of discipline are lovingly taught and carefully kept on a regular basis. These are some of my recommendations, however, specific details on all this can be found through Focus on the Family's website or publications.

> " *Goals are privately established together...to love each child with equal effort.* "

I am thankful that an early premise of this book about the five generations in America getting worse at parenting (Chapter 5) is countered somewhat by the stronger folks who get saved, discipled, and are determined to do things better with their own children. Many testimonies in Bible-believing churches in our nation prove this to be possible. When these regenerated adults find their proper purpose in life and work at building godly, unconditional bonds in the family, they will influence their offspring to love, care, and teach the future generations of children to love God and one another deeply as well.

Our Lord has special ways of doing things incredibly well in willing families despite our human faults. True Christian parents manage to work against societal odds and pressures and to learn from the mistakes of their own parents. When led by the Holy Spirit, they can break free from some sinful patterns they inherited and raise the standard for their own kids. The Lord wants to see a contrite heart from these Perpetuator-parents (Isaiah 57:15). Then the children will be able to watch and understand the grace and goodness of God operating in them.

However, to let God build trust and the ability to pardon usually means a total change of heart (or soul). It first means to recognize and realize the need of a Savior (Unit II). When a second generation parent is willing to turn to God and repent of his or her judgmental reactions toward mom and dad's sin, there is hope for the whole family. As God works through the member that He has chosen for change, progress will slowly take place. This is why we need to isolate the four roles kids play. *I believe a counselor with this teaching can zero in on that grown person's hurts and needs, then build a case for recovery of most victims of dysfunction. When we see how second-generation children wrongfully handled their abusive or negligent Originator-parent, we will know how and when to explain and apply agape love (Chapter 7) and Spirit-led forgiveness (Chapter 8).*

GOD'S GUIDANCE IN BUILDING FAMILIES

Here is a view of the functional family that author Reggie Joyner discusses as a key for a local church leader in being most effective at changing and guiding delinquent families. His ideas are about teaching willing parents how to look at the Lord's role in the way they train their kids to be mature and understanding young adults of the future.

We need to see the Family as part of God's design to demonstrate to a lost world just who he is. Our humanness becomes the platform from which the Loving Lord demonstrates his power, goodness, and love to people. God's plan is to do amazing works within the church and the home to put his Grace on clear full display.

The first priority of a Christ-centered home must be to establish a quality of relationship with each other that reflects an authentic relationship with Father God. The genealogy list in Matthew chapter 1 shows that every Hebrew family and every generation was connected to God's story. He used the family through the ages as the primary conduit (a timeless platform) to pass down His promises and commandments to the next generation. The heart of God was communicated mainly through the heart of the family.[27]

The Jewish "Shema" describes how to know the only God personally and deeply and to make HIM real via all the parent-child instructions from this true God. It is given to us in Deuteronomy 6. There Moses teaches the Israelites to press the Ten Commandments (Deuteronomy 6:6-22) on the minds and hearts of their children and grandchildren. He singles out four times a day when parents can do this. Pastor Joyner describes this as a rhythm. First, when the family is sitting together like at meals. Second, when you take the kids somewhere in the car. Third, at bedtime when talking about the good and bad of the day and praying together. And fourth, when they wake up and get ready for school and the day. God says it is dad's or mom's (or both) responsibility to talk

---

[27] Reggie Joyner, *Think Orange, Imagine the Impact When Church and Family Collide...* David C. Cook, Colorado Springs, CO, 2009, 47-48.

about the good things their Lord has done, or can and will do for and with them in the daily happenings of life.

Then in Deuteronomy 6:20 Moses says the kids will begin to ask questions about the meaning of the various testimonies and rules and will want an explanation as to why they are so important to them. The next five verses tell the stories of God's interest in, protection of, and provision for His people who love and obey HIM. We parents can tell our personal stories about our Savior's answering our prayers and supplying our needs in special times of our past.

Or better yet, we can tell of unique occasions where the kids were recently involved or aware of the Lord's giving the family peace or assurance of HIS presence in financial or emotional times. When told with sincerity and conviction, these stories and personal illustrations will stay with our kids for most of their lives. They will then have the opportunity to encourage the same lifestyle with their own children. Outsiders likewise will see God's heart being played out in relationships between parents and kids of all ages, as well as daily gracious occurrences between siblings.

SEVEN STRONG SUGGESTIONS FOR PARENTS

So, with God's role in families being established, let me present to you my viable solution for the grown children of dysfunction as they try to work better with their own young ones. I have compiled a list of seven different areas where children need special attention and detailed work to help them to be physically healthy, emotionally strong, and socially mature. The kinds of flawed parents we've looked at so far do not understand these necessary qualities or do not care about them. Perhaps they don't even know how to invest in these traits for their own flesh and blood. Let me show you the main needs of children in our society today that must be part of what I would describe as a "Functional Family."

> " *Flawed parents...do not understand these necessary qualities nor care about them.* "

These could be strong suggestions for us to share with parents looking for guidelines. Counselors could build these ideas into the four times families meet together each day.

1. Kids are to **be loved and accepted**. Everyone needs to feel love. God made us that way. Babies thrive when they are loved. A person's emotions are developed based on how they are treated in the actions of someone older. Sacrifice by another proves that children are worth building up. We feel valued when people spend purposeful time with us. In a functional home, parents sacrifice on purpose with a caring plan to teach and show love through the years.

2. Kids need **to feel secure and free from danger and threats**. If they are not safe, they may become fearful or angry or they may develop an attitude of self-sufficiency. Children should not have to worry about their needs being met or their safety handled. A parent is responsible to protect and provide. When children are forgotten or left to fend for themselves, they may resent the lack of care, or

they may find ways to survive on their own. Resentment brings anger and hatred. Self-survival builds selfish pride and a lack of respect for those who should have provided for them. When needs are met and safety is assured, children feel cared for and safe. They can develop confidence and inner strength in a welcoming, trusting, and orderly atmosphere.

3. Kids need **to be taught that they are valued and important to the group**. Something with value is something of special worth. Like costly coins or items in a treasured collection, children need to feel their parents would sacrifice for them and treat them the best they can. When everyone in the group is connected, wanted, and handled with special care, each person will feel appreciated as a valued part of the family. They will want to stay together and honor each other in every way possible. Teamwork at each age level goes a long way in showing love. (See Philippians 2:3) But care needs to be exercised so they do not develop a selfish drive that they are to be valued above others in the house.

4. Kids need **to see they have future potential and should be lovingly motivated to pursue it**. When they are treated with respect and honor, they understand as they grow older, what they learn and experience will be used to strengthen themselves and/or help others in society. If our children are important to us, we should encourage them to use their talents, personality strengths, and spiritual gifts for God and others in the family and community. Thus, they can discover for themselves that they were created by design and have been given opportunities to excel as a valuable person. But we must

be purposeful here so that we do not build up their pride in a selfish or negative way; and that we do not emphasize making lots of money and gathering many tools or toys as their main purpose in life. Honoring our Maker is the real reason we all were born.

Wise Solomon said it right long ago:

"He has made everything beautiful in its time. He has also set eternity in the human heart; yet no one can fathom what God has done from beginning to end. I know that there is nothing better for people than to be happy and to do good while they live. That each of them may eat and drink and find satisfaction in all their toil—this is the gift of God." (Ecclesiastes 3:11-13)

5. Kids need **to handle emotions and work for peace** in relation to one another. Feelings are important; and how we show them demonstrates our God-built emotions. We are made stronger when we use our emotions in praise to God and to build others up. But too frequently parents do not handle their own expressions or feelings well, so they think they cannot teach their children to do any better. Not true! We must always strive to do better; and the Bible says with God's Spirit we can develop the "fruit of the Spirit" for the best of emotions. (See Galatians 5:22-23.) Positive parents will talk about this, set goals and rules to develop better relationships in the home, and reward the children who work hard at it. Forgiveness is another important principle. When there is hurt in the household, someone needs to get the siblings together for reconciliation. The Bible teaches forgiveness in Ephesians 4:32 and elsewhere. Functional parents will seek help or prayerfully muster strength to follow those guidelines.

6. Kids must **learn responsibility, independence, and good decision-making**. As children grow older and understand their strengths, they should be shown how to handle life on their own. They ought also to be careful in what they say and how they conduct themselves toward others. Then they need to develop and maintain good habits like taking care of their own bodies, establishing a system of saving, putting away their small possessions, organizing their rooms, and pursuing chores and special help around the house. These practices are important, worthwhile, and productive. As they mature, they must learn to value honest work and find merit in whatever they make or purchase. Developing grace in how to interact with others will lead to a successful and fruitful life. Adults in the home must set a good example of these principles as they live in and outside the home.

In this chapter I need to add one more principle that encourages a "functional family" to be strong and healthy. I am reminded of the way the authors of Proverbs in the Bible take a few important items, then add one more to it. Hebrew scholars say his purpose is to emphasize the point by citing an additional thought to consider. Agar in chapter 30 goes from 3 "things that never satisfy" to 4. Solomon in chapter 6 verse 16 goes from six things the "Lord hates" to "seven that are detestable to Him." And so, I likewise wish to leave the impression here that there are certainly six areas a healthy family must concentrate on. Yet as I reviewed what I have written, I was given one more principle from the Lord that will early on build a stronger life in our children.

The six points I have expressed so far in this chapter are important physical and mental needs that children must have to find themselves and to mature through their journey to adulthood. But then, there is an equally important spiritual aspect of their progress. So, I see a 7th one as necessary.

7. Kids need **to be shown who God is**. Everyone looks for a higher power. The human soul longs to have someone supernatural to admire and depend on. We are born with an empty "love tank" that needs to be filled throughout our life. Parents have the responsibility to introduce their children to their amazing protecting Creator and loving Heavenly Father who cares for them more than they can imagine. To know HIM is to talk of HIM and talk to HIM. And we are expected to prove HIS love by the way we adults live with and for our own Lord and Savior.

CONNECTING THE SEVEN TRAITS WITH THE FOUR ROLES

Now with these special traits explained, you can see a clear difference in atmosphere and relationships in a dysfunctional home. Remember my definition? Dysfunctional family: **A household where harmony between the members is lost and relationships are distant, critical, and disturbing (even dangerous) and will likely stay that way**. The kind of harmony and relationships that children need can be built and patterned in any home where the Holy Spirit is the guide. As this unit describes, we *counselors again should look for ways to share the gospel as we give advice and encourage the hurt ones to not give up.*

So, with these seven mature and functional principles in mind, let's go over the "four roles kids are forced to play." With the family I have been using as an illustration (Jeff's family from chapter one) we should look again at the scapegoat, the mascot, the loner, and the hero. Imagine what could have been. Ponder with me what was missing. And look with me at positive principles that should have been applied to help these kids to get out of the trap.

The oldest daughter, the Scapegoat, needed principles #1 and #3 from her father as she was growing up. Since she was not accepted by her demanding dad as a person to be valued for who she was, she felt unable to please him and unable to build a solid relationship with the "head of the house." And although she got positive attention and significance from her mother, it was not enough for the creative mind who wanted to fix the problems in the home. Had she received the needed approval and effective time spent with a loving dad, imagine how her ideas and encouraging example could have made a difference early in the house that became very disruptive.

Now, can we dream a little about the difference that the Mascot of this house would have made had he been shown he was safe and worthwhile in how he expressed his positive attitude. "Kids need to feel free from danger" (principle #2). This oldest son was often afraid of his dad because he got the brunt of his father's anger. Had he been shown that the Bible says, "in your anger do not sin" (Ephesians 4:26), this child would have learned to laugh more, and to use his emotions (principle #5) to accomplish good family feelings at gatherings, special occasions, or even everyday encounters with one another. Balancing humor with frustration is a characteristic that mascots need, and God's Spirit can provide.

Then there is the second son, the Loner. He needed to feel safe most days also, and his pent-up dream to accomplish something special with his time could have been nurtured during his growing up years. Instead, his abilities and ideas were squelched by fear of his mean pop. A wise parent would have seen the potential (principle #4) of this boy to work with his hands, like his father. If the Loner had been shown he was wanted and valued (principle #3), he would have had the courage and determination to excel and do it outwardly. Instead, he was put down and criticized for his feeble attempts at personal creation or accomplishment. As a man now, he is a good carpenter and jack-of-all-trades.

And the Hero – he had independence, good decision-making, and responsibility down pat (principle #6). He strove for those things all his life to prove to Dad that he could do things himself and do them well. Jack could have experienced this if his father had only guided him with love and interest. But instead, this dysfunctional dad who could not trust people and wanted to be on top of things himself could never pass this motivation on to his children to build them up. Dad needed to be built up all the time himself and did not know how or why to compliment his own offspring. Courtesy, praise, and recognition (Principles #3 and #4) were not expressions or characteristics that dad could offer.

So, the hero got recognition from outsiders or through achievement at school. A stranger took him under his wing, and for a while made this child a ruthless businessman like himself. This bothered Jeff who thought his son was turning against him all the time. Now it was too late to teach him who God really is (principle #7). And since he had no respect for his earthly father, the hero could not comprehend how a Heavenly Father would come to his aid.

FINDING GOD'S DESIGN FOR VICTORY

A self-made hero can be a person to be admired. But inside he or she is a person of turmoil. They want to be applauded, yet they feel unworthy because of their unresolved inner anger, which continues until someone sent by God opens their heart and rescues them from their disruptive thoughts.

I read in Craig Groeschel's helpful book, *Winning the War in Your Mind*, a penetrating statement, "You cannot **defeat** what you cannot **define!**"[28] If we do not learn what the causes and origins of family breakdowns are, the relational disease in the house will spread. As *counselors we can now show our clients how to diagnose, start to heal, and even replace the scars and pain that selfish or unconcerned parents produce.*

Can we see how to find the Scapegoats in a dysfunctional family and then explain or even define, how they missed comprehending their own value in life? As a child, they were probably never given parental permission to offer their heart-felt ideas for adjusting to relationships in the home. Everyone could have worked together to overcome or defeat, the controlling or neglecting of the flawed parent, but they did not. They could not define the problem.

So now, when they come to understand these flawed issues, the scapegoats can do one of two things, or even both. One, make sure she sees the value and contribution potential in each of her own children. And two, ask God to give her the power to forgive her own parent for that failure. And then love that mom or dad with agape love and defeat the bitterness or self-pity that she, the Perpetuator, has tried to hide for years.

---

[28] Craig Groeschel, *Winning the War in Your Mind*, Zondervan, Carol Stream, IL 2021, 35.

The grown Mascot must understand that it is or was God-ordained for him to share his talents and emotions with the rest of the clan. This would be his role <u>defined</u>. He could have been encouraged by the less defective adult to defeat the fears and discouragement that he and his siblings were feeling. But the truth is, he too is still valuable to the rest of the family as a grown man. Now raising his own, he can look for the gifts God gave his descendants. Next, he can properly develop their personality for the future world around them. Plus, he should be willing now to allow spiritual leaders to help him or her (the Mascot) learn there is great security in discovering the person he was designed to be.

> *"...there is great security in discovering the person he was designed to be."*

Now the Loner can begin to heal by hearing that his parents did not try to help their shy-one to develop because of their own weaknesses, that is <u>defining</u>. His problems were not all his fault. Nevertheless, God wants to make the wrong right. The emotions of the Loner were needed in the family of origin, but life then was complicated partly through his inability to express himself. But now God can give him the strength to try again. At this more mature time of life, the loner can prove himself, defeating his fears. Siblings or nieces and nephews may be surprised at his recent noticeable accomplishments. Yet his self-worth will grow, he will see his potential and start to fulfill his dreams. He will be grateful for the opportunity to find himself. God's power in this new person will shine greatly.

And now for this independent Hero. If he or she does not receive much recognition or praise in the home, they will force the issue and demand some approval or reward. This will not only cause struggles with brothers and sisters, but the flawed parent will feel the need to over discipline them. Not feeling appreciated and being punished for doing what is natural, the hero will bitterly or angrily plan ways to get out.

Now as grown and with new understanding he or she should be able to figure out why the parent acted that way (define). He may start by rejecting our explanations; but perhaps with our prayer and additional spiritual help, the hero may think about this new knowledge for a while and sympathetically extend a pardon to his difficult parent. By comprehending mom or dad's personality, the hero might for the first time figure out why they reacted wrongly. If he or she hears from us how God made them individually, perhaps they will look to HIM with contriteness for their own sin. At this time, the once bitter younger adult should be able to recognize the family dysfunction and then repentantly ask the Lord for more help to finally defeat the curse they are living under.

So, with this new information, families that are not healthy and functional can come to understand that what they suffered under as a child or teen need not haunt or afflict them forever. Dysfunctional Families usually happen because of the sinful ways and selfish habits of Flawed Parents. Plus, the natural but wrong responses of kids develop from the four personalities they are forced to deal with. Without Christ their life will evolve into more chaos and additional hurt and pain.

In America broken families have become a national calamity, an emotional pandemic that affects not only the offspring for many generations to come but also the friends and neighbors around us. Unless we in the church, the spiritual hospital, can admit there is a serious relationship problem among us and a great sin-infected issue right outside our doors; this deterioration of people in the neighborhood will continue, and may even put out the light that that healthy and harmonious families want to display.

Believers of the power of Almighty God must show others there is a strong, proven solution. There is definite hope for getting out of the sick-bed and for overcoming the wounds that disturb, devalue, or depress the victims of childhood neglect, mistrust, or abuse.

> " *Definite hope overcoming the wounds...that depress the victim of childhood of neglect.* "

It is my desire to help develop spiritual physicians that can discover the disease of dysfunction by observing the symptoms from injured or ailing individuals living around us or even worshipping with us.

With the information in this book so far, readers can begin to befriend needy families, create plans to approach, lovingly share, and carefully explain to them how they can work through and overcome the unfair lot they have been dealt in life. Recognizing God's Loving plan for the family and the passing down through generations the need to show children how they were created in God's image - can go a long way in giving each person an understanding of his or her worth as an individual. Even if they have not discovered their reason for living and their unfortunate suffering, the Holy Spirit can restore them. *Then we could be used by the Lord God to turn the light on in their minds and help them determine to turn things around and make a difference from here on. In a future* chapter we will discover a tried and proven method for churches of all sizes to work out an effective ministry to dysfunctional families in their parishes and neighborhoods.

ROLES OF CHILDREN IN DYSFUNCTIONAL FAMILIES

	SCAPEGOAT	MASCOT	LONER	HERO
Positive traits	Fixer, Open, Planner	Comedian, Ease tension	Timid, Dreamer	Friendly, Determined
Negative traits	Easily disappointed	Impatient, Angered	Avoid family	Edgy, Retaliate
Lost thru flawed parents	Accepted, Valued	Security, Controlled emotions	Loved, Find potential	Appreciation, Spirituality
Finding what is missing	God's time, Parental love	Learn from trials	Feel God's personal love	Understanding, Sympathy
After spiritual commitment	Sacrificing for family	Finding future purpose	Defeating Fears, Helpful	Showing Grace, Forgiving

Here is the story of each of the roles dysfunctional children are forced to fill. I start with the good traits they were created with, and the negative ways the sin nature makes them react. The third horizontal row shows what they needed according to Chapter 10 "Healthy Family". This is what the FLAWED PARENTS could not provide each important personality. Then row 4 describes what they can find or learn once they are shown the issues of family dysfunction. The last row is the difference that Christ can make in their thinking, and more importantly, in their loving actions towards one another!

Chapter 11

POSITIVE LESSONS IN SUFFERING

We have seen how much the devil hates the family. We discussed how difficult it is to build a mature functional clan in a home because of sin passed down from flawed parents. But we have not yet looked closely at the glorious ways that a loving, sovereign God can put a broken household back together. Scattered pieces can be discovered, compiled, studied, and then, like a jigsaw puzzle, carefully and systematically lined up and put together the right way. Psychologists, family pastors, Christian counselors, and other earnest Spirit-led believers can use biblical insight to gather the strewn segments from a family hurricane. With God's guidance we local church leaders can snuggly fit and systematically reform a powerful picture of strength and beauty in a new household.

This reminds me of the old children's rhyme that talks about something big falling apart: "Humpty Dumpty sat on a wall. Humpty

Dumpty had a great fall. All the king's horses and all the king's men couldn't put Humpty together again." But God supplies the amazing power to reattach and rebuild. With man this is impossible, but not with God; all things are possible with God (Mark 10:27).

MIRACLES NEEDED IN FAMILY COUNSELING

If a godly leader can show a wounded second-generation couple why one or both have been ensnared by strong temptations, there is great hope for re-establishing the love lost in their own battered relationship. A Spirit-led counselor can also point out the negative and evil strongholds they have foolishly begun to believe. If we look at the testimonies of many changed lives both from stories in the Bible and in recent history and personal examples, we see that God is in the business of answering earnest prayers and altering losing outcomes.

But with the grand adjustments and victories won between former sparring mates, there is always hard and humbling work involved. It is mentally painful to admit our sin and apologize for it. It is also emotionally rough for the other partner to say "OK, I will accept your words and try to trust your sincerity. And I hope you will be able to forgive me my wrong as well." What earth-shattering emotions are felt here, and what pride-breaking decisions are made together in the hope that this colossal moment of reconciling and compromise will bring lasting results. Thankfully, it often does.

But I have also seen these momentous times take place in the counseling room only to discover days later that the promises were too difficult to keep. Later, someone still lost their temper in everyday situations, or one of the partners brought up another past crime that continued to tear them up inside. Then, it is seemingly impossible to put the pieces back together without a more serious dependence on the loving God they claim to know and want to honor.

It is only when a troubled, broken Christian is willing to fully focus on Christ's work for him and his shattered soul that genuine improvement can occur. Or perhaps it is when she concentrates on Jesus' purposeful sacrifice to make her whole or she suddenly feels Jesus' Spirit of love pushing on her crushed heart. Often reconciling begins when one side allows the Word of God to penetrate more deeply. It is one thing to know with the head what is right and wrong. But it is better when a sorrowful person allows the Holy Spirit to search their heart and show them that they are the one sinning the most not only against their distraught family, but more so against God.

> Have mercy on me, O God, according to your unfailing love; according to your great compassion blot out my transgressions. . .. For I know my transgressions, and my sins are always before me. Against you, you only, have I sinned and done what is evil in your sight. Psalm 51:1, 3

Then it is time for the humbler one to exercise their contrite spirit (cf. Isaiah 57:15) and accept God's work through the Word. It will show that less spiritual person how to change their thinking and to walk closer again with Jesus.

You may have noticed, also, that God often works with one adult at a time. The convicted one, with much prayer, a kind and forgiving attitude, and full dependence on the Lord, will become a spiritual light to follow. In time, then, through his or her persistence the opposing mate will frequently also be brought to the place where both will decide to do what is right. The emotional suffering they both experienced in putting their lives back together will have been worth it. Remember, trials produce perseverance, character, and hope (Cf. Romans 5:3-4). And the new character will impact the kids and grandkids for years to come. The curse of Deuteronomy 5:9 can be broken and altered for good (see chapter 1).

God is in the heart-changing business. And the people you are working with may very well be part of the miracle he wants to do next. Let me share a story that illustrates this point. I worked with a Christian man who had been in and out of church, caused a lot of drama in his home, and was addicted to marijuana. He was introduced to me in one of his sober moments, and I started to meet with him on a weekly basis. He wanted help with his lack of control. The first thing to do was to discover for sure whether he was a true believer. After two sessions the Scripture convinced him that he was. One convincing verse was Hebrews 13: 5 "Never will I leave you; never will I forsake you." Cory then had true peace and was ready to tackle the other issues that haunted him.

We worked on his past dysfunctional childhood and the broken home he had caused after marriage because of anger issues and drugs. Then came the feeling of distrust of God. The Lord was not making him stable and dry. I used many of the principles in this book to counsel him. Then I firmly warned him that as a Child of God he had to quit resisting the commands of Scripture because his Lord may be ready to just turn him over to Satan (cf. I Corinthians 5:5).

As that stark challenge burned into his soul, Cory decided to get serious. He spent much time reading and praying over God's Word. This led him to apologize to his wife and son for the damage done to them.

Next, he stopped hanging out with his addicted friends. Now he is a changed man. The Holy Spirit helped him to see that though he felt like an unworthy sinful person God still wanted to work through him to bring glory to his Lord. Now he is free from drugs and has fallen in love with his sweet, patient wife all over again. Cory is fully committed to serving his Savior and greatly desirous of seeing others saved, even family members.

FOUR GOOD ANGLES IN SUFFERING

So, with this introduction for putting broken families back together again, I believe that the Lord Almighty can use us to halt the suffering of many dysfunctional families in our neighborhoods. Let me next share a fruitful strategy that I have found to work in most trying circumstances where families find themselves. I would like to use the alliterative pattern of building on four words. Two words that help us understand some principles that will be effective in counseling aching families are PAST and PITFALL. Then two other words, POWER AND PEACE suggest additional positive ideas that help us to rebuild those who have become painfully dysfunctional. *Not to simplify a greatly difficult situation, but this compiles what I have said so far into a short summarizing process. It is important for those of you who are excited about this material to try to apply these four words in your counseling with dysfunctional family members.*

Past is for looking back with the purpose of building on our mistakes and the hurt others have put on us. Looking back can turn those hurts into steppingstones to bring helpful, lasting change. It is true we cannot change the past, but we can make peace with it. What others have done is under the bridge and down the stream. Many hurt people hang on to physical or emotional wounds too long. The more they think

"*True, we cannot change the past, but we can make peace with it.*"

about their unfair treatment, the more it becomes a mental stronghold that they can never talk themselves out of. Thousands of people in our country are struggling with past mistakes or childhood scars that make them feel unworthy of anyone's love. They have become emotionally damaged enough that they are convinced others do not want to get close to them. Isolation leads to loneliness, fear, and depression.

Without talking about their difficult experiences, the warped mind can sometimes cause a person to become bi-polar or schizophrenic. These acquired mental illnesses are often not dealt with until they are overwhelmed with worry and fright. I have seen teenagers who have developed such mental maladies because they were not loved and were regularly put down in their home. There are many adults who have been emotionally beaten down by grave disappointments or have been shocked by sudden losses. This brings on intellectual weakness or panic attacks, for which there seems to be no help or hope. As a result, we hear of confused veterans committing suicide, searching teenagers discovering the occult and demon worship, over-stressed sedentary workers going to psychologists weekly, the homeless population growing in cities, and tumultuous people becoming dangerous and committing crimes, even toward their own family members. Then also, in America now, we have crazed felons and angry illegal aliens being let out on urban streets.

Yet there is a godly plan available to help people in the early stages of loneliness and depression. Powerful verses in Philippians 3:13-14 show the steps to mentally allow the past to wash away. "Forgetting what is behind and straining toward what is ahead," Paul says is the way to keep the worries and fears from conquering our thinking process. He is not saying that forgetting is erasing the horrible experience from our memory. Rather it is realizing that as unfair and unreasonable as that bad occasion was, it will not be allowed to master us anymore (cf. I Corinthians 6:12.) *That is a choice God wants us to help the weakened Christian to make.*

The Father's plan to aid the sufferer is to train or adjust their wounded emotions in a positive way and cast their hurts and mistakes into HIS pool of love. The wounded believer can allow their Lord to replace their "stinkin' thinkin'" with acceptance. As Craig Groeschel says in his helpful book on stress and poor self-image, "They need to agree with what God says, and then claim that they are extremely significant to HIM."[29]

The Lord's feelings toward us are much more important than what others say about us. In time and after they have trusted HIM as Savior, this wounded person can press mentally toward a realistic goal of growing spiritually and becoming more like Jesus. They will realize that they owe HIM everything. Therefore, they can give HIM their attention, their worries, and at the same time their love. That is the prize Paul talks about (Phil. 3:14) that believers have been created and saved for, even called to. When the one with a changed heart refuses to let his or her past mistakes, feelings, and fears master them, they will experience a victory that the Lord planned all along to give them. Christian counselors need to find these misunderstood and misplaced individuals with hard to forget backgrounds before it is too late.

---

[29] Craig Groeschel, *Winning the War in your Mind*, Zondervan, Carol Stream, IL, 2021, 32

Note also that God can bring previous crimes to a just conclusion. If the believer repentantly leans on HIM, HE will make it right. Of course, dysfunction always causes pain. Most listening victims can then agree that the gracious Lord will miraculously and ultimately soothe that pain. If one really gives their hurt to God, HE will comfort. If in faith they allow God to have HIS way, HE will work justly on the family member who did the hurting. HE will be the holy, righteous Judge and make things right. Paul says in Romans 12:19 that his wrath "will repay the avenger." So, we are not to be the jury. Instead, we can walk today in HIS Grace and leave the past in HIS timing! Then move on.

> " *We can walk today in HIS grace and leave the past in HIS timing. Then move on.* "

Pitfall has to do with how far a person can be brought down when he holds onto his anger or self-pity. For some, it is like a very deep well they have fallen into, and when they try to climb out in their own strength or ideas, they get caught on dirty roots or sharp stones that will not let go and continue to cut badly. They are powerless to change until Jesus is allowed to come and help deal with the harm and the snares Satan caught the person in.

The boiling heat in a petri dish of a science lab helps to separate the dross from the real element. The pressure people find themselves in at times from trying to fix issues with their own reasoning or defensively denying their own sin - can become a serious spiritual crucible. The heat that the truth can put guilty people under can often cause sincere remorse. Godly pressure can also push folks to finally confess, and desire change or real cleansing. It is foolish to ignore the fact that God could be allowing someone to suffer in a trial so they will admit their fault. Then the Lord waits for believers to ask HIM to protect and carry them through the spiritual crucible. The embarrassment or regret from sins committed can force the bad feelings to the top. In the end, the troubled soul is refined like silver or gold.

This "crucible of grace" will turn things around. Sudden changes in the family with the Lord's help often do soften hard hearts and transform nervous emotions. Godly pressure can turn angry reactions into humble responses. The pain and misery felt from the heat of the Holy Spirit will many times separate, or push out, sin which is the dross. In Psalm 38:4-10 David describes pain and mourning, poor health, and loss of physical strength over personal sin. This passage also describes the harm that people working for Satan can cause, as God in HIS wisdom may allow. But when an afflicted person can talk to the Lord, he or she will find forgiveness and refreshment of soul (Psalm 32:2,5). No matter what parents have done to distraught children, or the grown victim has done to his own kids, it is more than possible with God's grace and love to be pulled out of the pit of bitterness, anger, fear, or regret.

Pitfalls, my friends, can be good for the perplexed. They may pressure them to repent. When a person feels sorry over his or her sin, the Holy Spirit will soon help them find sure triumph in Jesus and HIS understanding love (Psalm 32:5). So then, with cleansed hearts and clearer vision, positive things start to happen such as power and peace. They did for King David (Psalm 32:6, 7, 10).

Next for the victims of dysfunctional families comes **Power**. It is available to anyone who realizes the truth that they are very important to God. Then the person discovers he was designed to be set apart for the Lord, to be free from the control of sin and selfishness. The Apostle Paul tells Christians in Romans 8:12-13 they do not have to yield to or revert to the mistakes and habits of the past. Instead, the Holy Spirit inside gives him or her the power to put them to death. As they surrender more to God's way, HIS Spirit will take their hearts and spirits from being "friends of God" to "sons of God." They can hear "the Holy Spirit speak deep in their hearts" proving they are HIS loved children, and HE is their "Abba Father." They are "heirs of God and co-heirs with Christ" (Romans 8:14-17). To me that means that the saved individual will share in Christ's treasures, too. For everything God gives HIS Son will also be given to the true Christian.

In addition, this means that the saved one shares Jesus' suffering (arrest and crucifixion) and feels pain over their own sin. Then to some degree they experience Jesus' glory through their enduring obedience (Romans 8:17). So, they will know the power of being set free from the condemnation of their past and from living with the dross of the "old man" being in control! There is the great promise that selfishness and temptations to satisfy egotistic wishes will disappear. The believer then longs for something more and change is heavy on his or her heart daily. Thus, yielding to the Holy Spirit, and HIS supernatural power will cause the submitting Christian to reflect the Lord's glory and be transformed into the likeness of His Son (2 Corinthians 3:18).

All of us have the ability to demolish those stronghold patterns of wrong thinking and acting that have captured us for so long. We can now live with new hope and confidence. Our lives can be filled with wisdom that comes from heaven (James 3:17), which means attitudes that are peace-loving, considerate, submissive, merciful, and sincere. When we allow the Holy Spirit to take over in our thinking and living, we can operate with supernatural strength, forgiveness, kindness, patience, and even joy (Galatians 5:22). This is the fruit of the Spirit made real; God taking over in guiding us through victory in our lives.

The fourth "P" is for **Peace**. Peace comes when God's love rules in hearts and lives. The suffering ones are finally able to set their difficult offender free of the penalty they silently wish on that mean one. Before they can have this peace, they must exercise Christ's agape love. The former victim will now release the mental handcuffs that they had around the symbolic wrists of the person who hurt them. They will react in love and grace and then see peace come over both parties.

Everyone needs peace, but especially people of dysfunction caught in confusion and recipients of little love. Peace settles emotions and gives inner strength to continue within the complications that surround the hurt. The New Testament tells us that Jesus is peace. HE Himself is our peace who made both groups one (Ephesians 2:14 NASB). To know Christ is to know what peace is. To walk with Christ is to have HIS Spirit guiding and controlling the bruised one. So those who are at odds with someone or even enemies of a person can become a partner in the healing process just mentioned under "power." It is up to this victim to choose to trust God. If he or she will put the future in Jesus' hands, there will be a different result. The heart will not be troubled and there will be no reason to be afraid. "Peace, I leave with you; my peace I give you. . . .. Do not let your hearts be troubled and do not be afraid" (John 14:27). The trouble of the past will not eat away at them any longer. No

"*It is up to this victim to choose to trust God.*"

fear of unreconciling with family members or being unqualified in a parent's eyes will bother the cleansed soul again. The Savior will guide, open doors, and provide a way to stop all animosity. Trusting in HIM will continue each day.

*Pastors and counselors must share with second- generation parents (the Perpetuators) with whom we interact that their **past and pitfalls** can be overcome with love and forgiveness. And why not explain **power and peace** from the Holy Spirit to the children of dysfunction, pointing out that they can get rid of heavy hearts and decide to trust Jesus' peace for real victory?*

The aggressive **controlling and conforming** parents can be pulled out of the unsatisfying pit of selfishness and possessiveness. They were designed by God to lead their children and help them find who God wants them to be. Likewise, the **coddling and chaotic** moms and dads can see the need to repent of their giving up responsibility. Then they will see better how to love those special gifts the Lord has given them.

SUMMARY FOR SUFFERING IN HARD TIMES

In collecting all these thoughts together, we who are called to aid the victims of dysfunctional families can show them that:

1) When they are willing to cast their hurts and regrets on to God, they will begin the necessary journey to be able to emotionally forget and spiritually forgive what has been done in the past. (I Peter 5:7, 10).

2) As we help them to accept Christ's forgiveness for their sin, they will be able to recognize their suffering as experiences or pitfalls that God purposefully brought them through. Their terrible trauma can be something that purges their improper thoughts and shows them how to trust their loving Lord to give them a new triumphant life (Romans 5:3-5).

3) Now the Holy Spirit living inside their souls takes over (John 14:26). They have a new ability or power to think and plan freshly. Their emotions and reactions are different, more loving. They will begin to feel godly compassion for the ones who took advantage of them.

4) This new believer will from now on live with confidence that he or she is created new (2 Corinthians 5:17) and improved because of what Jesus did for them. They will be surrounded by hope and assurance that their Lord will always be there to help them to live better and in peace.

PURPOSE IN SUFFERING

I want to speak more specifically now about suffering. Some children have suffered mistreatment because the parent purposefully harmed them, others because the adult did not realize the various aches they were causing. Some parents deprive their young of a sense of security by not allowing them to see any hope of anyone coming to make things better. And even worse: to purposefully hide God's existence from children is a malicious act. Further, to never permit them to hear of or experience God's love for them is more than cruel. Some kids probably wonder why they go through loneliness or loss of care. Children can easily develop the impression that the Creator, like their own father, does not care about their feelings or future. Others are told there is no greater power outside their home to rescue them from abuse or pain. Still additional children grow up thinking that a controlling God wants their parents to over discipline or drastically punish them for wrongs they are told they committed. Sadly, it is no wonder teens are committing suicide at alarming rates all over our country.

But we have hope. "I lift up my soul to you O Lord. O my God, I trust in you... Let no one whose hope is in you be put to shame!" (Psalm 25:1, 3 KJV).

Perhaps we counselors can explain to the teen or young father or mother the truth that God is overwhelming love. HE loves them as they are and plans to help them get through their pain, confusion, hurt, and loneliness. Christ's wish for them is that they would learn of and adopt the great compassion and forgiveness HE has shown people in the past and has caused forty different authors to clearly explain in the Bible.

However, because of the Fall of man, sin in the world creates many perilous and unreasonable circumstances. People act selfishly, greedily, hatefully, and maliciously. So, the way individuals are treated is against the last six commandments of God (Exodus 20:12-17). Although often unrecorded, HE can and does protect many children around the world from serious accidents, mysterious pandemics, and cruel massacres; masses of innocent people are not spared. The Almighty does not choose to heal everyone. Even when Jesus, God's powerful Son, walked the earth, HE did not circle the globe and heal all the sick and demon-possessed living at that time. Suffering has always been in this world and always will be until the Millennium. Father God has also allowed millions of HIS Believers to be martyred down through the centuries, even babies and children.

So, when our counselees have suffered as children under controlling or manipulating parents, God was there. The physical injuries and mental damages were allowed in God's time for the future when someone would be sent to reach them with the Gospel of grace and the new power of love. *You the counselor may be that emotional Provider and spiritual healer that God now sends to this previously innocent child of dysfunction.* Because the younger ones needed grace and love, they can better appreciate and welcome it when it comes. Jesus explains this well in John 9 with the healing of the blind man. This handicapped individual was born, as you may remember, with a physical problem so that he could be healed and saved as an adult to bring glory to God in great victory over suffering. At the right period in the lives of the broken kids who became mascots or loners, God will break through with mercy and justice.

But then, there are times when it is necessary for fallen souls to reach out to the rescuing Holy Spirit or even a guardian angel that was protecting them from total calamity and drawing them to an affectionate Savior. Sadly many children suffering under dysfunction are kept from seeing this caring Helper and Comforter. (John 14). Or else they decide they do not want HIM. *Yet, we need to remind the victims that God will not give up easily. HE may additionally bring a caring mate or a friendly Christian acquaintance into their adult life to help them understand how to overcome their sorrow or anger. And perhaps, my reader-friend, you are the one useful to the Master and prepared to do this good work* (2Timothy 2:21).

We have already discovered that trials, temptations, suffering, and hateful pressure come to make believers stronger and to help them really see the Power of a merciful God. As referred to in summary above (See also section under Pitfalls), when they come to see they have been chosen, they permit the Holy Spirit to build in them perseverance and the motivation to keep going amidst serious trial (Romans 5:3-5, 8). Then HE will develop character in them, the quality of personality that will not blame others for their past dysfunctional experience. From this alteration of doing life comes hope which is the deep feeling that redeemed people have, no longer disappointed with their reason for existence.

The Maker has saved the seemingly unwanted person from their sin and graciously allowed them to see that purpose in life is to honor and promote such a Savior. Their hope is in Jesus. They now marvel at God's goodness. Then the soul who previously felt unworthy can rejoice in the way HE led them out of Satan's evil intentions of their suffering in a dysfunctional world. The "crucible of grace" has been good.

They now can be led into a new calling to not only stand for Christ but also to become ambassadors for the Son of God to other wounded offspring. As counselors are aware, 2 Corinthians 5:18-20 states that those who know the Lord are to represent HIM lovingly and honestly with the people they are around. This will enable those who have learned through unfair family suffering to be used by the Lord to perform the ministry of reconciliation. Those who have overcome past pitfalls can share their miraculous stories and through an explanation of the Gospel of Christ enable more people to be saved and strengthened.

THE CHOICE IN THE PIT

In the New Testament, James tells Christians that they are to face and then rejoice over the results of trials. Paul warns that when they choose to live for Jesus they will be persecuted. Peter says to continue to do good things when suffering under evil. *Past trials caused by wicked or confused adults should be used by the Lord through us helpers to show that bad things happen for a reason.*

And if the emotionally injured adult can follow the principles in this book, he or she will be able to overcome their pitfall in sin and work with the Comforter to find peace in their soul.

Again, Matthew 11:28-30 assures that if or when they take Jesus' "yoke", which is the power around mental and spiritual shoulders to lift someone out of worries and burdens, they will be given rest. HE is the power to make dead weight moveable. Remember Lazarus (John 11)? All who trust HIM can have their shame and guilt taken away by the grace of Jesus. *When we counselors teach those brought low to take on Christ's "gentle and humble heart" and stop feeling self-pity or unrighteous anger, then the victim of family dysfunction will be set free from life-long mixed emotions.*

Fellow pastor and counselor, focusing on what the LORD says will help our clients to break down all the strongholds they have in their minds. As you have seen, love conquers all sin. "The perfect love of Jesus drives out fear." (1 John 14:18) When the "hurt-ful" and "hurt-ed" are helped to fully love and trust in the real God, HE truly brings the victory. "Thanks be to God! HE gives us the victory through our Lord Jesus Christ." (1 Corinthians 15:57)

Chapter 12

UNITED EFFORT

If Christian leaders from around the USA would come together and strategize a clear way to help bring health and strength to dysfunctional families, we would see some profound changes in our society. Outside of another great awakening or national revival, that may seem foolhardy and impossible. However, we are told four times in the Gospel writings of the New Testament that nothing is impossible with God. The Holy Spirit could move on the hearts and souls of millions of Christians in America to consider and evaluate the problem and then to support one another in attacking it.

Three years before starting to write this book, God allowed me to experience the real agony and human trauma of several families being torn apart by the selfish actions of flawed parents and the frightening reactions of defensive children. The most obvious devastating issue that these families dealt with was drugs. With a few other community leaders, I worked tirelessly to help these broken families get out of the painful trap of addiction. We saw amazing triumphs in some of the individuals and a few of the children and parents came to rejoice in the power of God.

But alas, others walked or even ran away from the help we offered. In the land of the free and in the place where millions of gadgets make life much easier, we have allowed our communities to be broken from within. The prediction of the Russian leader Khrushchev 70 years ago, "We will destroy America from within" is coming true in our nation now. But just as we rallied together to win the Second World War and mustered to put the first man on the moon, our nation could still resolve to rebuild the most important thing, the Creator's designed family.

In this 21st century, groups of relatives living in the same house or apartment take many different shapes and sizes. These domestic gatherings should call themselves families even if they are not all blood relatives. Yet, on the other side of the definition of family, there are selfish and proud hearts who often try to push people away and out of a family. For when the Lord is not a part of such relationships, whether naturally born or circumstantially made, the families will quickly become unhealthy and dysfunctional. Psalm 127:1 says they are built in vain. But God has a plan for each of the wounded and lost clans living in our neighborhoods. And "HIS design for the family" needs to be carefully explained by a counselor; because taking the distressed individuals to church on Sundays is not enough to bring about the heart-felt change that is needed. Personal one-on-one teaching and being godly examples will often lead a person to decide on an alternate way of sustaining healthy families.

I know this firsthand, for a few years ago I felt led of the Lord to seek to revive a discouraged little congregation in a rugged suburb in

> " *God has a plan for each of the wounded and lost families living in our neighborhoods.* "

Pennsylvania. Before locking the doors and selling the property, we felt God wanted to put life back into the old church that had once served 250 people. Now, just a handful of weary folks held things together. After leading worship services for twenty stalwart believers for about two months, I noticed there was a lady who attended occasionally with her granddaughter. None of the regulars knew much about them, where they lived or what their personal relationship with Jesus was. I took this on as a challenge. Leaders of a local church are called by God to reach people for Christ and to give believers an example of welcoming others to be a part of what our great Savior is doing.

AN EXAMPLE

Building relationships was the first thing to do. I learned that the mother of MaryAnn, the young lady who came to church with Grandma, had practically abandoned her daughter. Grandma Christy's daughter was under the influence of drugs and was living with different men at various times. Christy was ashamed and wondered if the folks would accept her in the church. So, I set up a time when my wife and I could speak with her to offer help and give her assurance that we cared about them, and they would be welcomed. The counseling session went well. Grandma was open about her past and her current strained relationship with her second husband. She was waging a valiant battle trying to keep 12-year-old MaryAnn safe and to prove to her there was a much better way to live. Step-Grandfather was an alcoholic, so Christy was raising her alone on a limited income and in a chaotic atmosphere.

Bettie and I assured her that we wanted to help with these three concerns. And we asked permission to get the assistance of others in the church to provide material needs, teach MaryAnn about the Lord, and give regular counsel and a listening ear and loving shoulder to Grandma. Through the months several people provided special physical needs for a growing pre-teen. We started a Good News Club on a week-day afternoon to share the Scripture with MaryAnn and a few other children who lived in the neighborhood. Christy now felt welcomed in our church and was amazed at the things the people there were willing to do for them. She also came to our house many times for help to work through the stubborn and obnoxious issues that her ungodly husband was causing her. She also wanted advice on dealing with her distraught daughter and at the same time being positive with her granddaughter.

In time Christy grew spiritually. She had accepted Christ as her Savior as a young adult but never had the opportunity to learn much about Jesus and God's plans. She became quite vocal in her faith and praised God for answers to prayer and the difference He was making in her dysfunctional life – past and present. She eventually became a member of the church, was involved in various ministries, and was a strong testimony in the neighborhood and her workplace.

THE PLAN

Working with this family was a good example of the tried and proven 7-step plan for local churches to follow in meeting needs in dysfunctional homes. Several strong and caring believers among us helped to develop a program to reach other hurting single-parent moms and lonely and lost teenagers in our city. Let me share with you the details:

a) **building relationships** with the hurting
b) **offering** food, clothing, household items
c) **listening** carefully and sympathetically to these needy prospects
d) **counseling** biblically and providing applicable reading/video material
e) **working** towards a serious personal **spiritual** victory (salvation experience and discipling)
f) **encouraging** church attendance and **worship**
g) **providing** a form of continual **discipleship** training.

WORKING THE PLAN

Principles of Love (steps a, b, c). The folks at our church bought into this program. We touched many families around us. Even if they didn't regularly attend our Sunday services, they knew we cared for them. As a result, the folks who were blessed recommended others to come to us for the first three principles of love as outlined above. We had more than one wounded adult or hungry teenager visit us to get food from our Elijah's Pantry. Community leaders and even other churches worked with us in various outreach and counseling ministries. We had a vibrant youth ministry called "Ground Level." It was a monthly walk-in event that encouraged teens to come and play ping pong and other games, get a warm meal, hangout with friends, hear the gospel presented softly, and share their burdens and difficulties of life with casual freelance counselors.

A sidelight of interest: Halloween was a big family event in that section of Western Pennsylvania. Trick or Treat Night saw hundreds of families come out in the streets dressed in all kinds of costumes and fancy creations to encourage their children. So, we hosted great walk-through events in the basement of our church building with some scary displays, Bible character dress-ups, quick gospel presentations, and lots of candy and gifts. Each year before the City Council set the date, they would ask my wife, who attended most of the community meetings, when it suited our church to have Trick or Treat Night? They knew and appreciated the work our people put into this display.

I think our church grew in numbers because we realized that God was very much alive among us, and HE was providing for hurting people through our small group. Needless to say, several believers among us learned what it meant to be sincere givers (Acts 20:35) and good listeners, "Everyone should be quick to listen" (James 1:19). Dysfunctional families from the houses around our building were able to enjoy our safe place and experience the peace we were offering. We built trust with our community, and the borough leaders realized that we were interested in loving people. This unique consideration was noticed not only by those struggling financially but also by young and old who were wrestling

" We realized God was ...providing for hurting people through us. "

with domestic and social difficulties. Sadly, most of these folks would not even consider going to God or the church to get rid of the mental anguish they were experiencing. So, we found ways to go after them and to use this **7-step program** as an evangelistic tool without being pushy or condemning.

After a church establishes the testimony that they care and are interested in the outside people and what they are going through, the next step is for the church attendees to show that they will openly acknowledge their own struggles.

We have learned that our God has answers to help us cope with the sadness, disrespect, and harsh realities of life. And we have gone to HIM often to get the strength to go on and thrive in this world. As believers in Christ who know Him personally, we like to share with our new friends and neighbors what God has done and is doing in our lives. And it could be that the loving sovereign Lord has brought us in contact with them to offer help.

Counseling (step d). Here are four thoughts we have shared to help the needy person to handle the emotional trauma they are going through:

1) *God created them for a purpose* – HIS love includes an exciting, encouraging plan for their life (Jeremiah 29:11). "In the shadow of your wings I will take refuge till these calamities have passed (Psalm 57:1, NKJ). If they want help, God will provide it in time.

2) *Satan has caused their abuser or ill-equipped family member to thwart or stop that heavenly plan for their future.* "The thief comes only to steal and kill and destroy" (John 10:10), But Jesus is stronger than

the devil and the issues that chaotic families bring. "The One who is in you is greater than the one who is in the world" (I John 4:4).

" *Satan caused their abuser to thwart that heavenly plan.* "

3) *Sometimes God will allow hurt or harm for a period to show us* HE loves us and knows exactly how to get us through this serious interruption "Blessed is the man who endures temptation, for when he has been approved, he will receive the crown of life" (James 1:12, NKJ)). Faith can be built in a wounded heart.

4) *As we trust HIM, Christ will provide strength in special, surprising ways.* (See Matthew 7:7-11.) He loves to get involved in lives that are open to HIM. He longs to fellowship with people who will respond in faith. "God is faithful, who has called you into fellowship with His Son, Jesus Christ our Lord" (I Corinthians 1:9).

Perhaps the hurting individual can come for regular sessions where biblical principles are explained more through videos or discussion times. As soon as possible the Gospel of Grace needs to be explained clearly. The hurting child or confused young parent needs to be shown that Jesus was sent to earth and the Cross to wash away their personal sins with HIS Blood and then they should be given the opportunity to ask for God's forgiveness.

Conversion (step e – spiritual victory). When people understand for the first time that their stubborn, selfish heart can be cleansed and their loving Creator will no longer remember their mistakes or evil deeds when they repent, then the light turns on in their mind, and they realize they are set free from their troubling past. No matter what terrible things they have been told or forced to do, God will forgive and forget. "Because of HIS compassion and grace, God does not treat us as our sins deserve. Knowing our weaknesses, the Lord removes our sin as far as the east is from the west" (author's paraphrase from Psalm 103:8-13). Our sins are never to meet with HIM again!

The evil thoughts of revenge or the plots to harm others will all be erased from the all-seeing eyes of the One Who desires to be their eternal Savior. Assurance of personal forgiveness is a wonderful and powerful thing. Someone that important looks at them with great value, and HE wants to supply freedom from the misery and depression they have carried for a long time. *They need to hear this important truth from us* for God says in John 8:32 "When you know the truth, the truth will set you free" (John 8:32, author's paraphrase).

Encouragement (step f – worship). Likewise, a new believer needs to be able to respond to such mercy and grace. By attending Sunday morning services, he or she will see others honoring God for HIS great salvation. Christ's agape develops in the new believer a love for HIM and HIS plan to set him free. Freedom from past sin or pain enables us to talk and sing to Jesus more easily. We can open our mouths to thank, exalt, and praise the One who knows us personally and loves us fully. Worship becomes the opportunity for the new believer to join with others to express their awe and gratefulness for the change in their heart.

Discipleship (step g). Soon the person of dysfunction will realize that he is no longer an odd outsider. The role of the congregation is not only to welcome people they have never met, but also to help them feel they are part of the "Body of Christ". The new family members should not be judged, examined, criticized, gossiped about, or pushed aside. More mature believers need to arrange regular discipleship times with the new converts. And together they will learn from the Scripture and talk about applying verses to help them handle the struggles in life.

Satan, however, will try to get this person to return to the old ways or find certain things they do not like about some church members. Because we have been forgiven, we all need to forgive as well. But as mentioned previously, that is hard to do, and we must allow the Holy Spirit to help us totally get rid of pickiness or selfish preferences. Mentoring is essential for most young Christians, but especially those who have escaped from family dysfunction. Someone spending time with them in the Word will help keep the devil and his dealings (wiles) away. The more we study the Scripture the greater our love for Christ and HIS Word will grow.

A LIVING FREE MINISTRY

Now as I look back at all the common faulty methods of bringing up children we have described and the four main types of weak adults, I am really convicted that the defective parents we already have in our congregations need to be graciously told that they can do better. They should be shown that God can turn things around and keep them and their children safe in His hands. Some caring and experienced Christian leaders in the local church must lovingly explain to these parents that their philosophy of child-rearing has big holes in it. They must understand that they are currently allowing, even producing, dysfunction in their home. But God and the church people can show them a much better way.

I am hoping that my readers will see this colossal deprivation and determine to ask God to help them attack it with the people they are counseling. Can we not see the folks around us, even sitting in our churches, as Jesus described them in Matthew 9:36, "distressed and dispirited like sheep without a shepherd" (NASB Rev). We must have godly compassion for them, then sincerely and knowledgably start fervently to work in the harvest field, using the proposed plan we have just discussed.

There are loving ways to point out the fallacy of a person's lifestyle, especially if the flawed parents are born-again Christians. Paul challenges us: "(Each of) you must ... speak truthfully to your neighbor, for we are all members of one body" (Ephesians 4:25). *That hurting family we know could be much happier, and the future direction of the children could become more positive and hopeful - if we would allow God to show us how to approach the problem with grace. Many people we talk with every week need the Lord to show them that the indwelling Holy Spirit is "a deposit guaranteeing what is to come" to be far better than where they have been (2 Corinthians 1:22). This may give them the confidence they need to follow the material in this book as you present it to them. The Holy Spirit and His Word can fill in the gaps and give you the power to make a big Christ-honoring difference.*

There is one more factor we should consider at this point. We do not have to go looking only among non-believers to find families of dysfunction. As Living Free Ministries (LFM) points out, there are countless folks sitting in our churches every weekend who are victims of chaotic families and are not improving spiritually. In their research LFM has found undeniable truth that our congregations are made up of the 20%-60%-20% principle.[30]

---

[30] Jimmy Ray Lee and Dan Strickland, *Living Free Participant's Guide*, Turning Point Ministries, Chattanooga, TN, 1999, 8-9.

Here is what we learn: the first 20 percent are strong believers who are faithful attendees and workers. This group is excited about their relationship with Christ, and they work hard with the Holy Spirit to maintain strong relationships with one another in their home and church. Practicing agape love, they do not look down on others who are not as mature. They are heavily involved in ministries to reach the lost as well as to build one another up within the congregation.

The next countable group, the 60 percent, comprise the majority. They are usually born-again believers who love God and each other but are not as committed to their Lord or His church. They will come as often as they can and show up for the most fun and meaningful activities or one-day outreach events. They will likely serve on a few committees when it is convenient. However, their daily walk with God lacks vitality. In fact, many of the families hold secrets about their teens or their mates that they would not want to be known by the rest of the church. On Sundays they come with big smiles and positive greetings, even hearty voices to sing praises, but inside they are asking some deeply personal questions:

- Where is this joy that should be happening in my life?
- Why is my mate not trying to figure out how I am really feeling?
- When will my teenagers become open and truthful about who their friends are and where they go on weekends?
- How can I get my growing family back to where we were when the children were young, innocent, and obedient? Why do they argue and fight all the time at home?
- What is this guilty feeling when I try to worship my Lord?

This usually represents more than half of the body that you help to shepherd.

The other 20 percent are occasional attendees. These are the folks that are very broken, and everyone in the church knows it. They are the adults with whom the pastors, elders, and deacons spend most of their time. Some are in jail. Others are on drugs or alcohol. Couples are just barely hanging on to their marriages because they have been unfaithful, gambled their money, cannot keep a job, or just do not care about life or the Lord anymore. They are still members of the church or at least consider it as the place for their funeral.

The fact is, of course, that this third group needs the Lord to change their hearts. They have been dysfunctional for a long time, and they know it. The people in the first group should care more about what friends in the third group are experiencing at home. Perhaps you can encourage the spiritual folks of your congregation to be more involved in these seriously struggling lives.

Let us look closer at that second group, the 60 percent. These believers need to be reminded that God will give them more faith to believe He can change their difficult family situations. For they are dysfunctional too, but probably do not realize nor want to admit it. But if they will give themselves anew to Jesus in humility and earnestness, many of their doubts and worries and fears could be conquered. *Some willing and experienced folks within the congregation need to befriend a few selected individuals in that larger group also. These mature volunteers (not only local church counselors, elders, or pastors) could invite one of them to lunch or coffee and carefully and graciously ask some personal questions.*

- You do not seem to be yourself anymore.
- Is there something I can do to help with any issues you may be facing?
- Can I come over and talk about the troubling things that are happening at your house?

People are hurting among us every Sunday. Without judging them, we can ask God's Spirit to make us more available and open. It is not that we are blinded to our own issues, but we are becoming more open to sharing His love specifically with those believers that HE tells us to help. With our experiences and fresh biblical knowledge, we are desiring to be God's instruments to be used in a deeper, perhaps more concerned way than we have thought about before. Paul tells us that in a large house (perhaps a church) there are believers that God wants to use as "instruments for noble purposes". (See 2 Timothy 2:20-21.) *You counselors or assistant pastors or deacons can encourage these "gold and silver" believers to be "useful to the Master and prepared to do any good work" (v. 21).*

There are many dysfunctional families among us where we are serving our Lord. Maybe we have become aware of several wounded souls, sitting, and singing with us, who are unable to get over their pain. They go home every weekend still unhappy, trying hard not to show it. We spiritual leaders need to ask the Lord to show us who in our flock we can help. And we should ask Him to use this material, other resources, or even help from a parachurch ministry or Christian College on-line class to guide us in reaching out to those in need. We can love on, get to know better, care for, share with, teach, counsel, motivate, and disciple dysfunctional families.

We can help them on to victory in their lives and peace in their hearts. There may be many people just like Christy at your church, who wonder if they can be accepted and get some real help. Some in the 60 percent and the latter 20 percent groups of your church are waiting to hear from you!

UNIT V

SUMMARY FROM A PASTOR'S HEART

Unit V

SUMMARY FROM A PASTOR'S HEART

There are many obstacles that children in a dysfunctional home must face. More and more kids these days are forced to battle the drug culture - whether in the city or out in the country. I suggest that Elders and other mature outgoing Christians in a local church should be willing to get up-front and close with the struggling families in their churches.

In this Unit I talk about the Drug War that is waging in communities; and suggest some ways you can get involved to help families impacted by it. I also present a Five Step plan to work with either young people captured by various street drugs, or older folks clinging to opioid pain pills.

Then in Chapter 14 I seek to emphasize the importance of the role of a Counselor in every church. And when we have the talent and calling, we must be "faithful with the trust that has been given us" (I Corinthians 4:1-2).

Many of our friends and people in our congregations are afraid or ashamed to ask for help. God has called us to observe and work among them. They need a shepherd (Matthew 9:36-38). Your Lord can fill you with compassion and use you as a rescuer! This is my God-given passion! Perhaps you will catch it. Be your Brother's Keeper!

Chapter 13

WHY I WROTE THIS BOOK

As I said in my introduction, I grew up in a divorced family and developed a peacemaker personality. I am of a Phlegmatic temperament who responds with calmness and then seeks to make things easier or better for others. Experiencing dysfunction as a child, I can still remember the day my dad met with my sister and me to tell us about our mom's adultery. I was 11; she was 8! I was able to survive the shock and sadness with the help of loving grandparents and other caring friends. That is why I still have such a sympathetic heart for helping others who suffer from one or both parents who have wandered from their calling to raise their children well.

I have always preached and counseled with great compassion toward children who have been abused and neglected. I have also often discovered that when they are grown, they still struggle inwardly with bewilderment of who to trust and how to react when criticism or conflict occurs. And with childhood neglect there is the fear of still being unworthy or left alone by a relative without warning. This is what some psychologists call Post Traumatic Stress. *Loving and godly individuals must help these doubting souls to rise above the eruptive anger or silent depression that they experience in their mind and heart for countless future days.*

STREET DRUGS AND THE BREAKUP OF FAMILIES IN AMERICA

There is another reason I focus so much time on this important topic. I was greatly stirred in my last eight-year ministry at a small suburban church. There I found a sample of the severe trauma that many children of our nation are enduring because of drug and alcohol abuse. Several families around our church building were experiencing a very difficult life because a dad or mom was endangering themselves and their households by use of pain pills or street drugs. God had dropped my wife and me into the middle of a small cauldron of demons who were slowly and invisibly manipulating the destruction of a community. It took me a while to realize the evil that was surrounding us. Yet, I felt the Lord protecting, sustaining, and pushing us to take HIM at HIS Word. We were to build HIS Church there fighting successfully against the "Gates of Hell."

The folks of this old historic town were strongly Catholic, but unprepared to stand against the closing of their steel mill. Like many other communities the moral deterioration and the loss of the stability of the American Dream was negatively impacting the residents of the southwestern counties of Pennsylvania. Loss of work and idle time were ruining the psyche of the breadwinners. Because some dads were not properly protecting their families, Satan was making inroads all over our county.

During a period of six years, we learned of the difficulties behind the closed doors of many houses in our area of the city through the various church family ministries. Numerous arguments between dad and mom or teen and parent were getting louder and more violent. Police were often called to unruly homes. There was little opportunity for the restless teenager to talk with the addicted adult. Frequently, the ailing grownup was either angry, sickly, or emotional, and seldom at home. When a curious kid could find the parent sober and in a good mood, the mom or dad would not be willing to talk about the problems they had or the issues they were causing everyone else. Either mom did not know what was happening in the family or dad did not seem to care what his teen was feeling. By this time, the unaffected parent had given up on the marital relationship and had stopped covering up the blackouts, pass outs, and hangovers of the addicted adult. This frustrated parent, who needed more support, was often belittling the troublemaking spouse and turning the children against him or her.

In our children's ministry we saw or heard about the physical mistreatment of grade schoolers at home. We even reported one case to the authorities. In our youth programs we saw resentment and lack of respect toward stepparents and often heard about the lost love their mom had previously provided. Although the single parents of some broken homes appreciated the kindness and effort we gave to their kids, most often they did not want any help in dealing with their own chaos.

When we did get an open or welcoming response from a hopeful parent in a dysfunctional home, we were quick to jump on the opportunity to help. In chapter 12 we described the various ways that we as a church tried to open parents' eyes and provide answers through building relationships and then showing the power of Jesus Christ to change their crippled situation.

This regular interaction with families, often in their houses following a bad scene or tragedy, became as important to me as preaching every Sunday. I saw a lot of change in countenance and lifestyle with our team pouring themselves into the needs of the families around us.

I discovered several neighbors and a few church families who were secretly struggling with serious drug addictions. I wanted to do more than sympathize or give advice. I searched for a clear path on how to guide users away from controlled substances. I wanted to encourage parents to try lovingly but firmly to keep their teens from buying or trading meth or heroin with their peers. I educated myself on the overwhelming dominance that these chemicals had on the brain and passed the scientific and medical explanations on to anyone who would listen.

EXPANDING THE WORK

Then I realized the Lord wanted me to go beyond my local church and *work with organizations who were already fighting the battle with drugs.* So, in addition to preparing and preaching sermons each week, I joined local coalitions, attended community meetings, met with state and city leaders, rallied a couple of ministeriums, coordinated with several police

> " ... *the Lord wanted me to go beyond my local church fighting the battle with drugs.* "

and fire departments, and then became the chairman of the faith-based sector of the local County Drug Coalition. Through this effective organization we hosted community events and programs to make people aware of what they could do to help their loved ones or conflicted neighbors to get out of the trap of drugs. I even helped the faith-based part of this important coalition to write their own official purpose statement using scripture in the determined roles of government officials to attack the problem and rescue or build up the family victims.

- Mission of the Coalition: "committed to positive change and the creation of drug free communities across our county".
- Faith-based Purpose Statement: 1) strive to get free. 2) provide steps for lasting recovery. 3) reach for salvation of souls. 4) restore relationships at home and in the community.[31]

This group worked effectively with county schools, local businesses, government officials, the medical professions, and many religious organizations. Our goal was to educate and guide those under the influence of controlled substances, the parents and relatives of such victims, and the various police and fire departments of our area. We desired to make public streets and facilities safe, aware, and productive in curbing the devilish impact of drugs there!

Rallies at fire halls and small group Bible studies were two effective tools that several pastors and I used through a 501 C-3 organization we put together. Public meetings took place in the many small communities around us, inviting people to see what was really going on and exposing

---

[31] Cambria County Drug Coalition, 1 Pasquerilla Dr., Johnstown, PA, Winter 2018.

them to organizations that could help their families. We had persons in recovery share their Christian testimony, answered the people's many questions, and passed out literature to combat the issues that dependence on controlled substances had caused other members of the family.

The Bible studies took place in several locations throughout the city and in surrounding small towns. They were led by Christians from several different churches. The powerful material from Living Free Ministries was written for parents, siblings, concerned neighbors, teachers, civic leaders, and pastors affected by or concerned with the battle over drugs. The facilitator encouraged casual participation and openness of all who attended.

We saw much fruit from these events and became involved with doctors, lawyers, professors, radio personalities, police officers, EMT workers, nurses, morticians, and politicians. Some of our work prevented teens from dying, brought back young adults through Narcan rescues, and helped grieving families deal with unexpected fentanyl deaths. We encouraged parents to pay more attention and take their kids to rehab. Many of those affected listened to our gospel message and found Christ as their comforter and often their Savior.

Yet, we also heard sad stories of men and women who fought the help instead of receiving it. Others spent wasteful time in and out of jail and pushed their friends and loved ones away. We even had a shocking case of a young orphan rescued who was left alone in a house because the parent or guardian lost their battle with relentless addiction – and no one found them for 3 days! Our community teams of professionals and volunteers re-committed themselves to fight in the war to rescue families who were failing at life and losing hope. Or our workers were assisting and loving the confused children who did not know how to recover from the devastation of being alone and helpless.

This kind of woeful atmosphere and painful experiences challenged me to keep trying to help anyone that God brought to my attention. I was stirred to try to talk with distressed families, scared friends, or sorrowful adult neighbors who were asking heart-felt spiritual questions and wondering, "why this time, this way"? The Lord gave me the words to say and the compassion to express what the Bible says about life and death, causes and accidents, hope, and what to do next. It was a joy to see the Holy Spirit helping hurt people to accept HIS love and a better way to think after the solemness of someone important passing from this world.

GOD USES COMPASSIONATE HEARTS

I have always wanted to be a problem-solver. First it was in my own family of four kids that Bettie and I carefully and lovingly raised. Then in our neighborhoods where families were down on their luck or had accidents that had caused great disruption to the normal way of life. Building sincere relationships with others is the best way to minister. Jesus did it. So, in raising our own children we found it natural to get involved with community people and affairs. There were Little League games, PTO events, high school musicals, graduation parties, taking city kids to church camp, or feeding the hungry next door, all prime examples of how Bettie and I tried to turn what Satan was doing into a victory to bring honor to the Lord. As I said before, marriage counseling can

" *Building sincere relationships with others is the best way to minister.* "

be a big part of resolving family issues that personal sin has caused. In every case, if the Spirit would open the eyes of both or at least one of the partners to see their mistake, selfish act, or unkind words, then feelings could be reconciled, and love could be restored.

I could cite examples in each of the churches where the Lord helped me to find better reasoning for their difficulties and to teach forgiveness for the two disengaged mates. It always thrills my soul to see God pull people back together through a detailed applicable study of HIS Word. Then to pray that the Scripture will be "sharper than any two-edged sword, piercing and dividing soul and spirit, and will enable them to judge the thoughts and intentions of their heart" (author's paraphrase of Hebrews 4:12). Godly counseling is especially powerful when the Holy Spirit convinces broken families to be "put back together again" (like Humpty Dumpty in chapter 11). I have seen it happen many times in 45 years.

I have been convinced by God to share my experiences in this treatise so that you could have and give hope. I want to point out principles, examples, and biblical statutes that will help any reader to determine best practices in discussing and using the Word of God for "teaching, rebuking, correcting, and training in righteousness" (2 Timothy 3:16).

The following true story illustrates well just why I have written this book. Shortly after we moved to a small, struggling suburban church, the Lord brought two young children into our lives. We connected with their mother at a community event at the city park. The kids were energetic and active. They came to our summer Bible school and our Good News Club. Tyrone was 8 and Margie 6. Margie was athletic, competitive, and very talkative for her age. Tyrone enjoyed memorizing Bible verses; and though shy, he enjoyed a good contest. Both were a joy to work with.

We discovered, unfortunately, that their dad was addicted to methamphetamine. Mom was embarrassed and angry, sometimes taking her frustration out on the little ones. The children were growing up under dysfunction, and my wife and I took a liking to them, spending as much time with them as possible. They sang in our children's choir, recited Bible verses and special lines at seasonal evening programs, attended church camp every summer, and showed great interest in reading the Bible and telling their friends what they were learning. We went to their sporting events and bought whatever products they were selling in school contests.

In his drug history Dale had been through rehab several times and in and out of jail on three occasions. When I visited him in the hospital, he had shot up with something that almost took his life. As most addicts do, he denied there was a controlled substance in his body even though the doctor said they found it. Cheryl said she had enough and wanted a divorce. He wept in the hospital room, so I had to try to calm her and console him at the same time.

From then on, Dale was no longer allowed in their home. There was a restraining order, and visitation was supervised just two weekends a month. Poor Tyrone really missed his dad. Margie handled things better. But both were torn over how to love him, since Mom emphasized that their dad was a loser and did not really care about them.

Soon afterward, Dale had to go to County Court for breaking probation again. Knowing he was looking at a long prison sentence, he pleaded with me to write a letter to the judge, asking for leniency. After praying for two days, I composed such a letter and asked the judge, whom I had met before in another situation, to consider giving Dale another chance. This Christian ruler of the Court called me personally and said, "Your compassionate letter came to me a day late. Thanks for offering your sincere professional help, but this man went back on his promises too many times. He must take the punishment and the help that the justice system will provide. Perhaps you can minister to his ex-wife and two children while he is gone for the next five years!"

The kids had both accepted the Lord as Savior through our programs. Margie continued to be an honest and good-natured child. But her brother became bitter and argumentative both at home and at school, and he stopped attending church. Soon we left the city and lost all contact with the family. We still pray that God will turn Tyrone around as he becomes a young adult and send someone to show this rebellious young man that the shame of drugs and dysfunction can be overcome.

The work with broken families is hard and can be quite disheartening as well as miraculous. *Those of us who are committed to using God's word with sympathy and empathy, must keep giving and doing while we still have the physical energy and the emotional strength to be the Almighty's humble instruments.*

More understanding on the impact of drugs in causing Dysfunctional Families would be very beneficial. As you have read already, some parents battling controlled substances cause broken families (see chapters 2 and 11, also). Other somewhat healthy families are destroyed by the drugs their teenage kids get involved in. I have worked in both scenarios. Sympathetic teams have tried to persuade and pressure the captured ones toward long-term rehab centers. They constantly walked and talked with those attempting to recover. Plans have been set to contact and encourage them daily and to pray with them over the phone frequently. Serious attempts were made to keep our clients away from suppliers. We have sat through painful withdrawals, brought supplies and medications to jails, and simply just loved on victims fervently.

With all my experience and additional research, I've concluded there are basically five distinct factors a drug addict or alcoholic must accept in order to overcome his/her terribly powerful life-long habit. *I want to share these principles with you the counselor, pastor, and committed lay leader before I move on to the last two chapters.*

UNIQUE STEPS OF COUNSELING

Take note of my five strong recommendations in working with individuals caught in substance abuse:

1. Admit they have a **problem.**

2. Accept professional and supernatural **help.**

3. Acknowledge that **God** does **love them.**

4. Address how the loving Lord is **drawing them** to Himself.

5. Agree to **work hard** for victory.

The trapped person who is causing dysfunction in his/her family through use of a controlled substance must first "Admit he has a Problem." He may have many excuses or rational reasons for getting off the right path. *But God has brought you, a caring Christian, into his or her life to show that there is a better way to soothe emotional hurt or ease regret and stress. When they are hurting or down emotionally, they must be lovingly and resolutely told they are overly dependent on that substance.* It takes serious prayer and God's timing with strong, confrontational words to convince many drug users that they must get help! *The Counselor-Pastor can arrange for this, so that as soon as they say "Yes, I'll go," they will be transferred to a highly recommended facility for the educating and convincing that there is a way out of their trap.*

Then he or she needs to be willing to "Accept supernatural and/or professional Help." Our words of encouragement and sacrificial acts of kindness can aid the now weak individual to see some future light in the darkness. We described the way to freedom as a three-legged stool. One leg is rehab. A couple months of rehabilitation can change their atmosphere and educate them on the dangerous perils they are in. The second is medication which often is a needed short-term solution to redirect their chemically weakened brain. The third is God's timely Word that can lift their depression or discouragement. If the addict or alcoholic can accept these three ways of dealing with their problem, and systematically commit to them, victory often results.

If we can get the one who has become a slave to a controlling chemical to agree that he **can't beat it on his own**, the next three important steps become a saving and sustaining reality. Number 3 to "Acknowledge God loves him or her" is to assure them that HE designed them before they were born and cared enough for them to give HIS life on the Cross. Therefore, they are significant people, and their Creator absolutely loves them despite their tough issues and many mistakes. Scriptures such as Ephesians 2:4 and Romans 5:8 explain that Jesus can change us from sorry sinners to worthwhile individuals. God's mercy, though

" *... their Creator absolutely loves them despite their tough issues.* "

undeserved, gives us a new life. And that is not because we should have it but because HE wants to give it to us.

Point 4 is to understand that since they are loved by their Maker, HE is working on their minds and bringing amazing things into their lives to prove they are personally forgiven. *Plus, the Lord is supernaturally arranging for special people to meet, help, and talk to them - like you.* They are being targeted by a merciful, sovereign God. HE is "Drawing them to Himself" for their good, no matter what they have done in their past or how unworthy they feel. *With this special understanding they will be able to repent of their sin as we guide them.*

The last point to make is that as their faith grows, the Spirit of God can urge them to "Work Hard" at resisting, then replacing their habit with positive thoughts, different friends, and a designated period of restoration. These steps and programs of overcoming can bring total change; but it takes faith, determination, and a strong desire to have victory. Yet I do realize, that as Alcoholics Anonymous emphasizes, they are still susceptible to relapse at depressing or surprising times. They must still admit they are "a recovering addict"! So, we counselors should pray often, connect with the recovering one regularly, and caringly challenge the other family members to encourage this improving one to reclaim his personal value and God's redemption.

With these additional counseling goals, perhaps, I've reminded you again that the lost soul is worth saving. They are made in the image of

God. No matter how damaged or strangled the drugs have made them; GOD is GREATER! "Where the Spirit of the Lord is, there is freedom" (2 Corinthians 3:17). HE can transform that nearly snuffed out "image" into a renewed testimony of HIS glory. Just as the recovering person must push and strive with strength beyond measure to have victory; so, we workers for Christ need to follow Paul's admonition to "strenuously contend with all the energy that Christ so powerfully works in me" (Colossians 1:29). Let HIS Spirit tell us when and if to pull back and entrust the stubborn demon-oppressed addict's future totally to the Lord.

I am praying that Christ will have his way in your heart as you minister for HIM. Goodness most often wins. And GOD is GOOD. *The way and where that HE works may still be a mystery, but the rewards HE gives for our efforts are strong and true promises.* If we are seeking to build HIS Kingdom with "gold, silver, and precious stones," the testing fire at the Bema Seat in Heaven will examine our sincerity and motivations. We will then receive our Master's rewards. (1 Corinthians 3:12-14).

And in time we will lay the triumphant crowns at Jesus' feet in total admiration and thankfulness realizing fully that we did HIS work in much dependence on the Almighty Lover of souls. As Revelation 4:10-11 states so well, we will worship and cast our crowns before HIM saying, Worthy are You, our Lord and our God, to receive glory, and honor, and power!

Provided that we have been called to help broken families and have earnestly done our best following Christ's leading during the time HE gave us as leaders in HIS church; that verse is what we will be privileged to say in our celestial stay at the end.

Chapter 14

COUNSELING IS A CALLING FROM GOD

PUTTING KNOWLEDGE INTO ACTION

As you yourselves are aware, knowledge is good but usually not enough. I *have shared with you my knowledge and experience in working with dysfunctional families for more than 45 years.* Focusing on good personal connections has been a key to guiding hurt people into healing. *I have spoken on much of what the Bible says about relationships* and trying to avoid selfishness and controlling attitudes in living with others. But knowing what makes sense and has brought results *is not the same as rolling up your sleeves and diving into working with the people themselves. That is what proves those results.* I will explain this more in a few paragraphs.

You'll remember the story of Mary and Martha in Luke 10:38-42 and that Mary was complimented by the Lord for taking deliberate time to learn from HIM. Shortly after the miracle of her brother's resurrection, Mary put her new knowledge into action. She is the one who anointed Jesus' feet for His burial. In Mark 14:6, 8 Jesus told the crowd that she performed a good work by faith. James says faith without works is dead. (See James Chapter 2.) And Paul told the Philippians they were to "work out their salvation with fear and trembling" (Philippians 1:12). I interpret the "fear" as reverence to God, and the "trembling" as fully committing ourselves to HIM to do HIS business the best we can, even if we're nervous at first. For Counselors then, *reverence to God is demonstrated by their faith. Commitment allows HIS Spirit to work as we help our broken counselee to see that he or she can change. We put our knowledge into action.*

GUIDANCE AND GOALS FOR THE COUNSELOR

*Thus, I am asking you to use what you have taken in so far in your reading to serve Christ with dysfunctional families in the best and most effective way you can. So, to help you apply the principles I've explained, I want to remind you that I have also **printed in italics** practical helps that I believe you can employ to aid these families the most. In each chapter my advice on solving relational problems has been italicized. I pray you will be able to work these out in the lives you are dealing with for God's glory and for the damaged one's benefit.*

I also want to emphasize again that the first goal in working with dysfunctional parents or children is to help them become new people on the inside. Then after they are saved, life looks far different. The next goal is to help them mature as God's children on the outside. This means someone in the church must spend time with these new believers to show them how to make Christ-like decisions, how to wait on God in prayer, how to resist worldly temptations, and how to find confidence by reading and studying God's Word. This discipleship can also be done by your mature, believing team members who can share the Word one-on-one.

Of course, this takes time, hard work, and determination to stick with the plan God helped you to make with this new convert. Satan will be unhappy that he has lost a servant. He will do all he can to confuse and discourage the freshly changed heart from staying in tune with the Holy Spirit or following through with the ideas you have shown him or her. That is why Paul tells the Colossian believers to prayerfully stay with this grow-ing process "...teaching everyone with all wisdom, so that we may present everyone fully mature in Christ. To this end I strenuously contend with all the energy Christ so powerfully works in me" (Colossians 1:28-29).

If it is "Christ's energy" working "powerfully" through the coun-selor, the *devil and his minions will be stopped. We put forth the earnest effort, but it is God who provides the supernatural power to make it hap-pen according to HIS will. If we are called to work with a unique disciple who had been a victim, we must recognize the spiritual battle that wages inside the new believer's mind. Again, the experienced Apostle states,* "The weapons we fight with are not weapons of the world. On the contrary, they have divine power to demolish strongholds (2 Corinthians 10:4). We discussed this in detail in Chapter 10.

Readers, elders, counselors, I believe there can be a victorious outcome for every victim that God brings into your life. Christian counseling is a powerful profession that gives more help and impact than most realize. It is also a clear personal calling from our Lord to use HIS righteous principles and commands of Holy Scripture in a close, specific, caring way to change lives for eternity. We not only take a person from the kingdom of Satan to the Kingdom of Light (Acts 26:17, Ephesians 5:8);

"*Christian counseling gives more help and impact than most realize.*"

but we also can set them on the path to be lights in the world (John 12:36) for the lost and the carnal to see (Matthew 5:16). Plus, we can be the "salt of the earth" as we provide heavenly taste for those growing in their faith and becoming strong testimonies of Christ's power (Mark 9:50).

I want to also highlight the use of small groups or recovery teams to help people you are counseling. Gathering three to ten individuals together to discuss and encourage folks of broken families, all at one time and place, is a great tool. Your clients will find additional people who are unfairly dealing with similar difficulties to their past life. It can be life-changing to see that they are not alone in this particular fight! When others begin to share their stories in a desire for the hope of victory, the empathizing and teaching of a trained leader will often encourage them to open up as well. Dr. Janet Lerner in her excellent workbook, *Restoring Families*, describes well the many benefits of meeting together in a small group.

By talking about the events and feelings of the past we are bringing them out to the open where the light of the Word of God is able to dispel all lies and heal the pain attached to them. We are not creating negative emotions, for the negative emotions are already there. By bringing them out into the light of a supportive, godly environment, we remove the power they have on us. We can be set free from their binding effect. We do this because, although the past is forgiven and covered by the blood of Christ, often it is not surrendered nor forgotten and needs to be dealt with.[32]

Counseling with the aid of others with similar issues is a powerful way of "strenuously contending" (Philippians 3:13b) to bring hopeful people to "become fully mature in Christ".

So, I'm glad you picked up this book; and hopefully you are, too. Let us remember James' warnings about teaching and knowing. The word "teach" in 3:1 admonishes us that we are to be careful what we say and then practice in life what we teach in discipling others. In James 4:17 we are reminded that to know what to do is not enough. We should listen closely to the Holy Spirit, so we use our knowledge at the right time and place. To delay or postpone too long can just be another way of proving "faith without works is dead."

LOOKING BACK AT A BATTLE WE LOST

That brings me to some unfinished business in this book. You will recall at the end of Chapter 2; I told a long story about a Coddling Mother with whom we were making great headway. But on Christmas Eve she was arrested. Quickly the family we were helping to nurture and get established and move along in faith was suddenly broken apart. Our growing opportunity to touch and disciple them stopped.

Following my theme here of hands-on effort after gaining insight on a tightly wrapped dysfunctional problem, I believe we were overly confident as a team in what we had done to help. As I ponder more on the situation, I also feel the devil temporarily won that battle for the souls and lives of those two teen girls because we did not do enough; we had

---

[32] Janet Lerner, "Restoring Families", *Facilitator's Guide*, Living Free, Chattanooga, TN, 2000, 6.

delayed. Granted, we never know when tragedy or accident will strike. However, this disappointing case reminds me of two verses about the urgency and intensity of time. I share this with the humble acknowledgement that we did not always properly allow for God's timing.

In James 4:13-16, we are told that we have no control over time and are dependent on the Sovereign One to show us when, where, and how to do HIS bidding. In Ephesians 5:15-16 we are told that we must be alert and wise about how we use our days of ministry. Our enemy is using his demons to change our plans when we are not thinking about the invisible spiritual warfare that is constantly happening around us.

So, here is what our church team could have done better with Sherry's dysfunctional family. First, we could have spent more specific and loving moments with the older daughter who was afraid to go to school or inexperienced to do what was best for her. She was that Loner personality (Chapter 1). We were getting close with the acts of kindness we were showing her. One of our ladies could have made the time to counsel her about how important she was to God and us. We told her that in a variety of abstract ways; but we could have explained more, asked God for the right words, prayed for her protection from the demon of poor self-worth, and invited her to go shopping or to dinner with us. We could have gotten to know her better and welcomed her conversation. She was in her room alone most days and had to listen to her parents argue and fight. Had I been thinking with urgency, these suggestions would have been a wiser use of time before that fateful day.

Second, we should have had more specific discussions to help Mom learn how to trust the Lord for things out of her control. We should have been alert when her Sunday attendance was becoming lax, and we knew she was spending more time with her unsaved friends than with her newer Christian friends. We were all very busy with our families, jobs, and church responsibilities, and December is full of many other things. Yet, we realized later that our priorities were off; we did not pray correctly about our schedules, and we did not see the warning signs.

Third, I had heard from neighbors that the abusive husband was heavily addicted to meth, but I sensed he was not as antagonistic towards us as before. He had noticed the way we were sacrificially showing love, providing food, paying some utility bills, and treating the three women as important individuals like no other church or group of people had done. So, I could have visited him and tried to build a relationship with him. Though I was constantly helping other people around the city with addiction problems, I had never discussed drugs with this man who ended up with an overdose (near death experience) at home on Christmas Eve.

Finally, it is one thing to know a lot about drugs and family problems, but it is another step to daily seek the Lord for wisdom and direction on what to do with that information and desire to help. Knowledge is not enough. Wise deeds must follow! Now, I am not trying to be hard on myself. Nor do I want to make this kind of ministry to families seem overwhelming or impossible. But as Jesus said in Matthew 9:37, "The harvest is plentiful, but the laborers are few." *We must earnestly pray, asking God to send out true workers to reap the harvest. We should ask HIM to show us if we are to be one of those needed workers.* HE will give

"*Knowledge is not enough. Wise deeds must follow!*"

to disciplers, guides, and peacemakers the strength and opportunities to do good.

If we are going to be involved with hurting homes and train others to do the same where they are sent, then we must believe that HE will use us. As trained laborers, we should allow HIM to show us how to be available to do HIS work. Paul again admonishes us to be filled with the Spirit because, ". . . (HE) is able to do far more abundantly than all we ask or think, according to the power at work within us" (Ephesians 3:20, ESV). *So, it is HIS power, HIS will, and we are to be HIS warriors.*

I am not trying to pressure you, or make you feel like you're being disobedient. I am simply reminding you that the needs are great. You could be one of God's peacemakers. As Luke 10:6 suggests, there may be a person of peace in the dysfunctional family you are working with, and your peace may find a resting place in his heart (soul). He or she may have been waiting for you for a long time. You may be the one God uses to heal an emotionally sick soul in that house who, in turn, might then represent the Kingdom of God for yet one or more additional people in that broken family. You may be the one God is preparing for "such a time as this."

A SPECIAL LOOK AT TEENAGERS

Before I close this topic of additional help for counselors and church leaders, let us zero in for a moment on dealing with teenagers. I am not writing as an expert on youth ministry, although in my six different congregations I have willingly spent much time loving on, relating to, advising, and just "hanging out" with kids from ages 12 to 20. So, I have learned some valuable lessons about how they think and the struggles they experience. In addition, Bettie and I learned a lot raising our four PKs. The first three energetic and creative girls were born in the 70s as

"Baby Busters". Then 14 years later God surprised us with a wonderful son. He was our "Millennialist", quite different from his older siblings, not solely because he was a male either.

Teens are not as difficult to guide and train in biblical ways as many senior citizens, non-Christian adults, and stand-up comedians try to portray them. Each generation has its own unique problems and frustrating challenges of correction or persuasion. Yet the majority of kids raised by stable and caring dads and moms still become respectful and responsible young people. When they are brought to youth groups in churches, they have a much greater chance of being positive examples for their unchurched peers and of responding in Christ-like manner to the temptations and dangers in their world. Please note again the hows and whys of "Functional Families" in the American society described in Chapter 10.

However, there are those teens who seriously resist the teachings of the Bible and who determine to live their lives, sowing wild oats and "grabbing all the gusto" they can get. This can happen despite the good influences around them at home or in church. Even conservative, well-established community organizations like Christian YMCA groups, or instructive athletic clubs and teams for children and teens can find their programs and events frustrated by angry or rebellious kids.

Many evangelical churches are faced with worldly, rebellious, or just plain attention-seeking kids who use vulgar language or start fights even in church. With manners and morals diminishing in public school, the leaders in churches need to get updated instruction on how to outsmart the troublemakers or how to prayerfully win them over with Christ's sacrificial love.

But I would like to suggest here that we consider that the real hidden reason kids act up or are resistant to our advice these days is that in many of their homes they are not cared for, are ordered around, disrespected, beaten, or even abandoned and living in enormous poverty alone in an empty house. They may have been or are being mistreated by one or more of the four kinds of flawed parents who may be worse than we have described. A survival-of-the-fittest mindset breeds impurity, hatred, discord, jealousy, fits of rage, and witchcraft (cf. Galatians 5:19-20).

It would be good foresight for Youth Pastors or seasoned youth leaders to get prepared for unexpected disruption of unruly teens at their meetings or events by going over the material presented in Chapter 8 on forgiveness, Chapter 9 on strongholds, Chapter 11 on suffering, and then Chapter 7 on "Agape Love." This teaching will clearly help to handle the lost teen who has been battered for years. Plus, there are many high schoolers who have accepted Christ at church who need to learn to forgive and pull down strongholds. They are struggling with great unhappiness at home from unkind words or actions of troubled parents who are not believers.

Leaders should have answers for the Christian teens to understand what has been happening in their unfriendly households. The four chapters just mentioned can help older kids rise above their emotional suppression and the Deuteronomy 5:9 curse. Perhaps working through these principles with the parents would be a good idea for a leader to do in a classroom setting, or one-on-one time, or in a small group. Many of our precious teens have no weapons of defense against the "friendly fire" attacks they have experienced or are still battling in their own strength. They desperately need peace. They must get to know Jesus better; HE is their Peace. HE is the answer for them to really ponder on and then make real in their lives.

SOME SPECIAL COUNSELING NEEDED IN HOMES OF ADOPTION

I also learned something in a Trauma Conference for parents who foster or adopt children. There are many secrets of abuse or neglect in small children that have long consequences for when they develop into the adolescent or teenage years. Many kids have decided in their minds to resist and challenge the acts and words of love that new moms and dads wish to give the children now under their care. Because of their previous mistreatment they feel they do not deserve any sacrificial love. So, they determine to fight the kindness and tenderness of their new parents. These untrusting children will lie to, steal from, deliberately disobey, even purposefully hurt the feelings of those adults who are trying so hard to love them.

Psychologists and professional therapists call this common issue RAD = Resistive Attachment Disorder. When this difficult child becomes a teen, he or she will have desired for family life to become unbearable for all involved. As he continues to feel unworthy, he will become mean and callous with peers also. Not understanding love, nor allowing himself to feel or experience it; he has perversely decided that no one else around him should have love either.

In this painful case the unstable teenager is the one who caused the family dysfunction, not any flawed parent. Yet, this family needs help just the same! Perhaps the youth leader can supply the parents with these suggestions for such a mental-emotional problem. Christ can help the weary, confused mom to counter such antagonism with tough love and determined fair consequences. And the wise dad can lead in a strategy to never show anger towards this child and always plan ways to have control of the problematic issue that the perplexed young mind tries to cause.

This troubled youngster needs to see that he is valued by God. His poor self-image must be altered to one of great worth, because he was created by a loving God in HIS own image! The worn-out adoptive parents need to get support from others so they can show this rebellious young person that they will be cared for and encouraged no matter what. These loving parents are interested in him/her despite the many attempts to block their affection and tenderness. The adults must not give up or change their minds! *As a church leader you could show determined dad and mom how to constantly ask God for grace and inner strength. In one way this fulfills the Lord's Scriptural promise as it relates to this mentally stubborn child* – "I will never let you down, and never walk off and leave you!" (Hebrews 13:5b, MSG)

Again, you could be the "peacemaker" for the victims of dysfunction. Two New Testament verses challenge us with the pacifying work HE can do through us. "Blessed are the peacemakers, for they will be called children of God" (Matthew 5:9). "Let us therefore make every effort to do what leads to peace and to mutual edification" (Romans 14:19).

Chapter 15

A RESCUE MENTALITY

As I close this project on aiding dysfunctional families, my mind keeps going back to Jesus' reaction to masses of people. I have always considered Matthew 9:35-38 to be a very mind-stirring passage. Whether thinking of HIS tireless traveling and preaching, HIS great compassion for people, or HIS command to pray for workers in the harvest field, it is clear to me what is important to Christ should be important to each of us!

Matthew says that when Jesus scanned the crowd of people, "He had **compassion** on them." When I looked up that word in the dictionary, I found this definition: "the sympathetic consciousness of others' distress together with a desire to alleviate it." I think of Jesus not only recognizing those with physical problems but being able to study individuals and know immediately their mental and spiritual problems as well. HE had a genuine desire to relieve each person of all that was keeping him or her from being complete. The passage implies that Messiah either understood their facial expressions or read their minds. Jesus saw them walking around "like sheep without a shepherd." They had no direction, no security, no answers!

The full meaning of God's compassion for people in Matthew 9:35-38 is avidly described by many different words in the various New Testament translations. The King James Version says they were "fainted and scattered," the New American Standard uses "distressed and dispirited," and the New International Version states "harassed and helpless." The New Living Translation goes further with "because their problems were so great, and they didn't know where to go for help." As we combine these narrations, we understand that Jesus felt their pain, empathized with their dilemma, and wanted to see them recover.

> " *Jesus felt their pain, empathized with their dilemma, and wanted to see them recover.* "

It is also clear in the Old Testament that God had great compassion on the Israelites. That is stated over and over despite their sin. In the book of Jonah God directed HIS merciful concern toward the wicked Ninevites, to the missionary's great disappointment. In the New Testament Gospels compassion for lost people is linked with Jesus nine times. In addition, Paul challenges us three times that we should especially exercise such sympathy toward other believers.

SEARCHING FOR SIGNS

Have you ever sat on a bench at a mall and watched the people go by? Or scanned the multitudes at a high school or college football game and wondered where each person stood with the Lord? Jesus looked at the multitudes on the hillside and not only taught them but fed them. I am reminded of Willie Wilson, a billionaire businessman in Chicago, who, at a time of extremely high gas prices, out of sheer kindness, generously gave $1,000,000 to spread over several gas stations. That way countless Chicagoans could receive free gas for a day!

As mature believers in the age of grace, we ought to be able to read the faces in our neighborhoods or churches and consider what we can do to alleviate their distress or helplessness. This is compassion that develops a "rescue mentality." As we intentionally make new friends, we should look for clues that reveal family issues are the cause for their disappointment or discouragement. *With the tools you read about in these chapters, you can not only desire to alleviate their distress but also effectively put forth the effort to remove it.*

GOD MAKES US WILLING AND WORTHY TO RESCUE

In *Rebel Without a Cause* Franklin Graham, son of evangelist Billy Graham, described his rebellious streak as a teen and college student. At that time, he wanted to see what he could get away with by pushing his mischievous behavior to the edge. Finally, he began to mature in the late 1970s and was greatly moved by the compassion of evangelist Bill Pierce. This tender-hearted man had a deep desire to come to the rescue of masses of people suffering through floods, fires, hurricanes, or tornadoes that suddenly ruined their communities and families. The self-centered son of the world-famous evangelist began to realize that a fulfilled life was not about what he could do for himself, but rather what he could do for others in Jesus' name.

As Franklin was prayerfully seeking the Lord about becoming involved with World Vision, its leader died. The WV board searched for a new director for a year, even though Mr. Pierce had told them he wanted Franklin Graham to take over for him. Some thought Billy Graham's son was too young, and others felt he was not mature enough to lead such a worldwide organization. Yet during that same year Franklin turned his future over to God and spent time traveling and aiding in devastated places around the globe.

One day a prominent pastor approached him with an offer to take over the helm of World Vision. Franklin said, "How can I know if I'm worthy of such an immense and sacred position?" The experienced warrior for God explained "worthy" as being ready to give oneself fully to the Lord. "It is better to be worthy before God and not have World Vision, than to have the direction of World Vision and not be worthy. Franklin, do you have the 'Guts for Jesus first?'" After pondering this for a few days, Franklin responded, "I am ready, willing, and worthy through Christ." He was accepted by the Board, and at the ripe old age of 28 became their new director.[33]

After a few months he expanded the part of Samaritans Purse and has emphasized this ministry to saving lives from international diseases like AIDS, Ebola, and Corona. Emergency portable hospitals were set up in various places in the United States and around the world. In addition to the medical help and to rescuing and restoring of communities after national weather disasters; suffering people also receive prayer and

---

[33] Franklin Graham, *Rebel Without a Cause*, Thomas Nelson 1995, 170.

the powerful gospel message. In addition, Samaritan's Purse worked with many local churches in Ukraine at the writing of this book to feed and relieve those enduring the ravages of war. Franklin's ministry also spreads much love to impoverished children around the world at Christmas time with the shoe boxes of gifts, small toys, and sanitary items called "Operation Christmas Child." All these gracious acts of compassion are from thousands of people whose hearts inspire them to be the arms of Christ in rescue.

These types of missions model how people can give of themselves to deliver those who are in great need. Like the good Samaritan in Jesus' story of Luke 10:30-37, we are likewise to have mercy on our neighbors. From that Bible parable we learn of this compassionate foreigner who picked up the wounded person in dangerous territory, gave him special medical aid, transported him to a place of charity, paid for his care, and returned later to minister even more. He had the "rescue mentality." Jesus said this kind individual knew what it meant to love his neighbor. We have many neighbors around us in America who need great physical, emotional, and spiritual help, especially victims of dysfunctional families.

There are children all around us who are being neglected and abused. Jesus said in Matthew 19:14, "Let the little children come to me, and do not hinder them, for the kingdom of heaven belongs to such as these." These innocent minds are open to new things, and their wounded hearts are looking for sincere love. Christ challenges us to welcome a little child in HIS name (Matthew 18:5) so they can be rescued by the gospel and be brought into the Kingdom of God.

Such is the role of people in an Evangelical Church. Such is the goal of a leader in the Family of God. Even if the entire dysfunctional family is

"Such is the role of people in an Evangelical Church."

not won to Christ, at least the little ones can be. Experts say 70% of all conversions in the USA are of children under age 12. *You, my reader, can play a significant part in carrying spiritual seed and sowing it. For, as we share Jesus' love with children and mothers through our various ministries, we will* "return with songs of joy, carrying sheaves (souls) with us" (Psalm 126:6). In addition, Solomon says, "He who wins souls is wise" (Proverbs 11:30, NKJV).

Thank you for reading this book. May God send you into HIS harvest field with an excited heart to rejoice and worship like the angels do when someone receives Christ as personal Savior. Remember, "There is rejoicing in the presence of the angels of God over one sinner who repents!" (Luke 15:10). May this be a big part of your motivation as you seek to rescue families in your neighborhood. Be your Brother's Keeper!

END NOTES

Chapter 1

1. Jimmie Ray Lee & Dan Strickland, *Living Free Participant's Guide*, Turning Point Ministries, Chattanooga, TN, 1999, 33.

2. National Institute of Mental Health Report, Depression Overview, nimh.nih.gov, June 1, 2022.

3. Interview with Dr. David Van Dyke, Wheaton College, Wheaton, IL, September 2020.

Chapter 2

4. June Hunt, *Dysfunctional Families – Making Peace with Your Past*, Aspire Press, a division of Rose Publishing, Inc., Torrance, CA, 2014, 35-36.

Chapter 4

5. *Zondervan Encyclopedia of the Bible, Volume 3*, Merrill Tenney, editor, Zondervan Publishing House, Grand Rapids, MI, 1975, 58.

6. Robert S. McGee, *The Search for Significance*, Rapha Publishing, Houston TX, 1990, 41.

7. Interview with Dr Thomas Edgington, Grace College, Winona Lake, IN, August 2023.

8. Janet M Lernar, *Restoring families*, Facilitator's Guide, Living Free, Chattanooga, TN, 2000. 11.

9. Janet M Lernar, *Restoring families*, Facilitator's Guide, Living Free, Chattanooga, TN, 2000, 3.

10. Robert S. McGee, *The Search for Significance*, Rapha Publishing, Houston TX, 1990, 103

11. Robert S. McGee, *The Search for Significance*, Rapha Publishing, Houston TX, 1990, 108

12. Dennis Prager, Prager U Fireside Chat #248 "Self Love vs. Self Respect", July 28, 2022.

Chapter 5

13. Forbes Magazine, Saul Gourani, November 2019.

14. Chris Segrin & Jeanne Flora, *Family Communication*, Routledge Pub., 2004

15. glennbeck.com "*Discovering Black Lives Matter Plot to Destroy the Family*", Glenn TV, Blaze staff, July 16, 2020.

Chapter 6

16. Henry Cloud & John Townsend, *Boundaries*, Zondervan Publishing House, 2004, 35.

17. Robert S. McGee, *The Search for Significance*, Rapha Publishing, Houston TX, 1990, 41

Chapter 7

18. Speaker Stacey Gagnon, Trauma Conference by Lost Sparrows, Warsaw, IN, September 2023.

19. Gary R. Collins, *Family Shock*, Tyndale House Publishing, Carol Stream, IL, 1995, 55-57.

20. Gary R. Collins, *Family Shock*, Tyndale House Publishing, Carol Stream, IL, 1995, 218.

21. Tim Jackson & Jeff Olson, *When We Just Can't Stop*, RBC Ministries, Grand Rapids, MI, 2011, 8,9

Chapter 8

22. Liberty Illustrated Bible Dictionary, Thomas Nelson, 1986.

23. Phyllis Jenness, *A Witness to God's Grace*, Gloria Gaither, "What My Parents Did Right, Howard Publishing Company, West Monroe, LA, 2002, 162-164.

Chapter 9

24. Dr David Irvine, *"Introduction to Chemical Dependency"*, Addiction Seminar, University of Pittsburgh in Johnstown, Johnstown, PA, Summer of 2019.

25. Dr Tony Evans, *30 Days Overcoming Addictive Behavior*, Harvest House Publishers, Eugene, OR, 2017, 7.

26. Steven Huff, *Speak the Truth in Love*, Gloria Gaither "What my Parents Did Right", Howard Publishing Company, West Monroe, LA, 2022, 145-146.

Chapter 10

27. Reggie Joiner, *Think Orange, Imagine Impact When Church & Family Collide,* David C. Cook, Colorado Springs, CO, 2009, 47-48.

28. Craig Groeschel, *Winning the War in Your Mind*, Zondervan Publishing, Carol Stream, IL, 2021, 35.

Chapter 11

29. Craig Groeschel, *Winning the War in Your Mind*, Zondervan Publishing, Carol Stream, IL, 2021, 32.

Chapter 12

30. Jimmie Ray Lee & Dan Strickland, *Living Free Participant's Guide*, Turning Point Ministries, Chattanooga, TN, 1999, 8-9.

Chapter 13

31. Cambria County Drug Coalition, 1 Pasquerilla Drive, Johnstown, PA, Winter 2018.